THE
EDIBLE
CITY

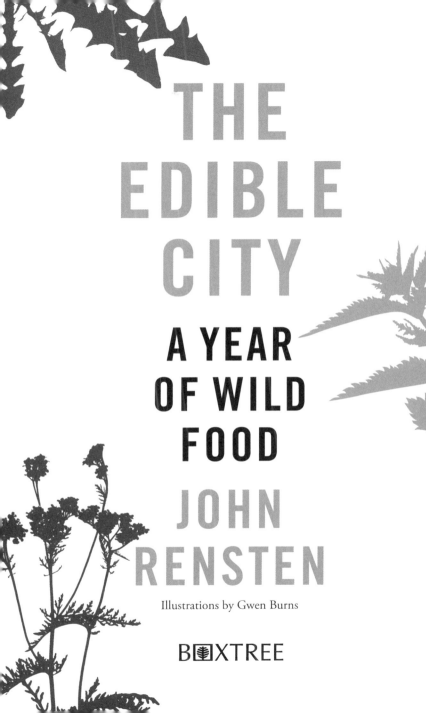

THE
EDIBLE
CITY

A YEAR
OF WILD
FOOD

JOHN
RENSTEN

Illustrations by Gwen Burns

BⵘXTREE

First published 2016 by Boxtree
an imprint of Pan Macmillan
20 New Wharf Road, London N1 9RR
Associated companies throughout the world
www.panmacmillan.com

ISBN 978-0-7522-6613-8

1 3 5 7 9 8 6 4 2

A CIP catalogue record for this book is available from the British Library.

Typeset by seagulls.net
Printed in Italy

Visit **www.panmacmillan.com** to read more about all our books
and to buy them. You will also find features, author interviews and
news of any author events, and you can sign up for e-newsletters
so that you're always first to hear about our new releases.

For Mary, Ellie and Oscar

Contents

Introduction

I can think of nothing more fulfilling than cooking with food that I have foraged. To feed yourself and those you care about with ingredients sourced by your own hands is to rekindle a relationship with nature, and the simple act of gathering our own food is the way man has existed for the majority of time on this planet. Although this isn't an activity that most people associate with living in a twenty-first-century city, I'm sure this book will change the way you look at where you live and allow you to share in some of the wonderful edible experiences that the city has to offer.

It was almost two decades ago that I was properly bitten by the foraging bug, and since then not a day goes by that I don't pick wild food, study wild food and generally obsess about all things related to wild food. I love sharing what I've learnt, running urban foraging walks, taking groups mushroom hunting in the countryside or combing the seashore. For eight years I ran a busy restaurant and revelled in the task of sourcing wild ingredients from outside the city to add to the menu. Eventually I realized that my greatest foraging pleasures were to be found far closer to home and turned my focus onto the place in which I lived.

Don't be concerned if the idea of eating foraged food in the city feels unsettling at first (take a look at the section on page 261 where we go through all the dos and don'ts, common-sense rules, safety, hygiene and legality to put your mind at rest). I'm certainly not advocating that you *only* eat foraged foods – even I don't have time for a totally wild diet. I fit the majority of my foraging into short bursts, shoehorned in between working and looking after my young son. Rather, I want you to see how foraged foods can make an incredible addition to the sorts of meals you are already cooking and eating.

More than simply the good eating it affords, putting on your foraging goggles will transform your city surroundings, from somewhere to be hurried through, to a place to be lingered over. Where previously you'd notice a patch of stinging nettles to sidestep, I want you to see the opportunity to make delicious wild tempura; rather than avoiding that tree that drops annoyingly sticky petals on your car, I hope you'll spot the chance to make a spring blossom champagne. And that clump of weeds – it doesn't need clearing, but rather identifying and then incorporating into some wild spring rolls or sushi.

Time spent foraging is as relaxing as it is absorbing; like taking a deep breath, it can bring a feeling of calm to an otherwise frenetic city. Simply walking from my house to the nearest station has become a voyage of discovery, a multi-sensory experience and a treasure hunt, during which I find myself smiling rather a lot.

The standard definition of foraging is this: 'the act of looking or searching for food or provisions'. The basics are simple and easy to learn, with a good sense of smell being more important than the ability to memorize hundreds of Latin names and complicated plant diagrams. My approach is to take the tiniest bit of knowledge and put it to multiple uses; so simply being able to identify a dandelion will provide countless, year-round foraging opportunities and produce culinary delights as diverse as a caffeine-free coffee, a mid-summer wine, roasted winter root vegetables and spring salads, all from just one, very easy to identify, common as you like, 'weed'.

You can use this book however you prefer; read it from front to back, all in one go, or dip in sporadically when you have a free moment, heading for the current month, or just pick an ingredient or recipe at random and modify it to suit what's in season or whatever you currently have access to. Necessity is often called the mother of invention, but availability, for foragers at least, is where the real inspiration lies. The type of cooking that comes from using foraged ingredients is naturally creative, inventive and ad hoc. These won't be the kind of recipes where things are always measured precisely; 'a handful' is often about as accurate as I get.

There are no real rules, other than avoiding the plants that aren't edible or for whatever reason are not safe to eat, but with enthusiasm and some common sense, a magical side of the city and its hidden larder is waiting to be discovered, probably right on your doorstep. I hope this book takes you on your own food journey, even if it just means you pay a bit more attention to the plants in your local park. With a little effort, it will allow you to begin viewing the city as I do, as a constant source of wonder, an ongoing education and a provider of almost daily inspiration. If foraging teaches us anything, it's to enjoy and celebrate what is available, not to hanker after what is not.

Where to forage

I live in London and much of the foraging I describe occurs there, but the majority of the plants I pick are in no way specific to the south-east or even the UK. Almost all of them are freely available across northern Europe, actually right across the northern temperate zone, which spans the globe, taking in countries as diverse as North America and Japan. Every country has its own common or local names for these plants, in fact most of them have many variations, so I've supplied the Latin names, which are always useful to refer back to in case of any confusion (pages 247–50). Once you start to look, you'll see the real problem is not finding food to forage for but choosing between so many options. On a spring walk through the unremarkable city park nearest to my house I can easily find lemon balm, spearmint, primrose, white nettle, poppy and yarrow growing at my feet, while above me are avenues of mulberry, hazel, elder, linden, cherry plum and hawthorn trees. Is my local park a particularly outstanding place? Well, yes and no. It has all the things I look for: a mix of well-kept and clean areas, combined with some intentionally 'wild' patches and a few less-intentional ones, interesting tree planting and a decent-sized lake, pond or waterway (the border of which is not overly managed). Basically it ticks all the foraging boxes but is no different from another hundred city parks I can think of, so for me, my local park *is* outstanding, not just for my purposes but for the many other ways in which it provides for the local and wider community.

From this one square mile of almost central London, I have identified, collected and eaten nearly 200 different edible plants, many of them giving me multiple crops spread out across the year.

In this book, I take you in detail through sixty of the most common and tastiest, but I reference many, many more.

The plants themselves fall into two, totally non-botanical groups. First, the genuine wild plants, unconcerned with the patchwork of grey blobs that make up the view of London on Google Earth; they are opportunistically able to grow anywhere, colonize a patch of turned-over soil at a moment's notice or barge their way up through cracks in the pavement. Wild plants don't need looking after, don't need feeding, pruning, watering or tending to in any way; robust, hardy, militant, were we to cease to be, I have no doubt that they would reclaim the city at a startling speed. The second group are the 'unintentionally' edible or medicinal plants, favoured for planting by both current and Victorian park and town planners, often forming entire avenues of trees or huge lines of bushes. The end result of all this intentional planting – coupled with the prolific growth of wild plants and feral/garden escapees, all thriving in the microclimate that is Greater London – is a huge area of natural diversity, as fertile and bountiful as anywhere else in the country.

Once turned on, your 'green vision' will be impossible to turn off; otherwise neglected street trees will suddenly bear fruit, patches of previously irrelevant land will become focal points and the city will reveal a network of free, edible treats, coming and going throughout the year. Things are never as they seem at the first glance and to really see what is in front of us, we need to learn *how* to look and what to look for. Do this and the buildings, the cars, the streets and the shades of grey will all fade away to be replaced by a vibrant, fertile landscape, full to the brim with sweet smells, strong flavours and bright colours.

Why forage?

Why indeed, should we be interested in eating any of these plants, with so much food available to us in the city? I can think of a hundred reasons, emotional as well as physical, and most of them will crop up repeatedly in the pages of this book, but for now, let's just look at nutrition and a simple, irrefutable statement of fact. Wild food is superfood. To clarify this it's important to define what's actually meant by 'superfood', especially as it's one of those popular terms that get overused by companies trying to market 'healthy' foods. It gives you some idea of how far the food industry has wandered from the path these days that the notion of food being good for you is a distinct selling point, rather than a given. At the same time, 400 generations of farming and a global obsession with growing and eating grains has left us with food that travels well, lasts ages, resists bruising, looks amazing and very often tastes of little to nothing. Since the mid-1950s, when the responsibility for processing and preparation of the majority of our food began to move out of the domestic kitchen and into the hands of big businesses, we have become ever increasingly separated from what we eat. The points of origin, provenance and methods of creation are often unknown and the techniques involved in turning the raw produce of grains, fruits, vegetables and livestock into the meals we ultimately consume are, to most of us, very mysterious.

Furthermore, the vitamins, minerals, proteins, nutrients, fibre, antioxidants and thousands of other phyto-nutrients (more about these later), have been bred out and replaced with our favourite legal high, sugar, to the point where the vast majority of the fruit and veg available to us is utterly stuffed with carbs, and not much else. I'm not claiming this is all the result of a huge global conspiracy – at least it wasn't initially – it's just that we like sweet things and as a result we have favoured varieties that give us what we want. I know a respected botanical nutritionist who describes sweetcorn, a plant, like so many, that bears utterly no resemblance to its ancestors, as 'Nature's own Mars Bar'. But then again, we wouldn't want to eat Neolithic sweetcorn, a tough and stony little thing.

Fortunately, like traditional hunter-gatherers, we can go back to nature, where all the wonderful nutrition we need is still waiting for us in abundance and all we have to do is take it. When people talk about a 'superfood', what they're referring to is anything that is extremely rich in minerals and vitamins, particularly beneficial to health and which contains much higher levels of antioxidants and enzymes than other foods, hence being excellent at supporting digestion, promoting healing, detoxification and nutrient absorption, aiding fertility and maintaining general good health. A few of the very common ingredients described as superfoods that are available in the shops include garlic, blueberries, rose hips, dark leafy greens, turmeric, cinnamon and flax. These could be joined by another fifteen to twenty items that are part of our commercial food chain, but were I to write a list of wild superfoods it would be pretty much endless. It's not that I'm anti mass-production; when massive cities have massive appetites, I appreciate that the food has to come from somewhere, but when over 60 per cent of the world's calories now come from just four crops (wheat, corn, rice and potatoes) isn't there room for some more variety in our diets, regardless of the apparent range of choice available to us in the city? Obviously these are big issues, where the problems and their solutions are political, and this is a wild food diary, not a selection of hidden agendas, so I won't be climbing onto my soap box . . . much.

All wild food, however, is superfood: nettles are over 30 per cent plant protein and full of iron and calcium; rose hips have, weight for weight, twenty times the vitamin C of oranges; hazelnuts have five times the protein of eggs; and just one teaspoon of seeds from ribwort plantain, probably the most common and widespread plant I know, has as much fibre as a whole bowl of porridge. I could go on (and on), but none of this would be of much use to anyone if the wild food we picked and ate didn't taste great, and it does, it really does. If my years running a busy London restaurant taught me one thing, it's this: flavour is king, and if your ingredients already taste wonderful, then simple cooking and good presentation are really all they need.

How to forage

'Grazing' is the loose title I have given to what I do in the city; sampling numerous plants, herbs and other wild foods, but mostly in small amounts, experiencing new flavours and learning how these change with the seasons rather than trying to gather armfuls of one plant when it's at its best or most obvious. The city parks and pretty much all of our urban green spaces are not common land, but privately owned and managed areas that we are allowed access to, and, leaving the politics of land ownership aside, if we want to forage in these areas, we must respect this, just as we do numerous other guidelines that allow us to coexist in such close proximity to so many other people. Obviously, it's up to the individual, but this is my take on how to treat these places, not to ever take for granted the effort that goes into making them as wonderful as they are.

On all of the foraging walks I organize, the idea of taking whatever knowledge we already have, however small, and gradually adding to it through gentle repetition and multiple encounters with the same plants, is a recurrent theme, a process as far removed from academic study as I can make it. Learn just two or three new plants a month, all of which will have multiple crops and overlapping seasons, and you have access to nearly a hundred edible wild foods, spread throughout the year. My strategy is to make a small amount of knowledge yield a big reward. Through this simple approach I've learnt more about nature, foraging, botany, nutrition, ecology and numerous other topics from the one square mile of city greenery that makes up my local park than I have from the rest of the entire country. And how? Proximity and gentle repetition, that's how. I find it slightly corny to call foraging an art but it does take a very specific skill set, best learnt over an extended period of time, and although later I'll help you learn to identify fifty wild edible plants in just ten minutes (that's all the UK's wild members of the Mint family), this knowledge is the culmination of numerous other things, including many repeated visits to the same places, passing and observing the same plants in all their different stages of growth, the changes of the seasons and how these affect what is, and what isn't, available.

Take this approach to learning and I guarantee you will simultaneously learn *how* to forage, to become aware of the seasons, the 'micro-seasons' within them, and to look at the city as a network of periphery, borders and edges, not just blocks of adjoining land but overlapping environments that offer increased diversity, fertility and opportunity. Once we can ID just a small selection of plants and become familiar with them, their habitats and the visual and physical changes they undergo throughout the year, we reach a point where the botany is almost irrelevant and what remains is a form of recognition akin to spotting a good friend a hundred feet away in a crowd of people.

When we start to investigate the extraordinary array of wild flavours the city has to offer, it soon becomes apparent that rather than living in a place where food remains separated from our day-to-day environment, we are actually surrounded by it: tasty, healthy and hiding in plain sight. Nature not only becomes a vast impulse-purchase section, but one where everything is free and the products are healthy and nutritious. The lemony tang of wild sorrel, the sour-sweetness of wild plums, the joy of finally beating the squirrels to a few hazelnuts and the sheer delight of tasting the first lime blossoms of the year – it's all there for us, it's free, it's fun and it's absolutely delicious.

January

Spelt risotto with roasted winter veg
and dandelion rosettes

The mighty wild green smoothie

Winter cress, wild garlic and chorizo soup

Crab apple fruit chews with sea buckthorn and star anise

Spring rolls with Japanese mahonia flowers
and wild salad leaves

*'The "winter greens" were flourishing: cow parsley, yarrow,
white nettle, mallow, garlic mustard and numerous others,
all producing lush leaves. Apparently, they didn't get the memo
saying it was wintertime . . .'*

DANDELION
Taraxacum officinale

Bright yellow, many-petalled flowers

Stems produce white latex when broken

Leaves with deep, roughly triangular lobes, often pointing downwards. No hairs

PARTS USED: Leaves, roots, flowers

HARVESTING TIP: Cut the top of the roots below where the leaves join to keep them together

3rd January. Highbury

Today was very chilly, the sort of cold that seems to creep under your clothing regardless of how many layers you have on. I took a stroll around my local park. The trees were mostly bare except for some crab apples, but plenty of 'winter greens' were flourishing; cow parsley, yarrow, white nettle, mallow, garlic mustard and numerous others, all producing lush leaves. Apparently, they didn't get the memo saying it was wintertime. As a result they were all happily getting on with their business and behaving like it was the middle of April, some were even having a go at producing flowers. While the plants might have thought it was spring, the weather certainly didn't, so with this in mind I was after ingredients for something hot and hearty. Many of these winter leaves are great as salads or blended in smoothies, but more likely at this time of year, I use them as cooked greens or in soups.

Also dominating the area were hundreds of lush-looking dandelions. Although they lacked their familiar yellow flowers and the fluffy seed heads that kids use to tell the time, they were still easy to identify with their distinct 'lion's tooth' leaves (hence the name, from the French, *dent-de-lion*) and were growing in plump rosettes all over the ground. Dandelion leaves can be really quite bitter, an acquired taste I'm not that fond of, despite their enormous health benefits, but finding them, as I often do, growing in longish grass, the bottom few inches of the plant had been 'forced' (meaning that very little light had reached the base of these plants and they had been unable to photosynthesize), so instead of getting their nutrients from the sun they'd pulled them up from the soil. This absence of chlorophyll makes them very pale and much less bitter, just how I like them.

Dandelion root, washed, gently roasted in a low oven for a couple of hours and then whizzed in a grinder, makes an excellent coffee substitute, but today was not a day for digging, with the ground as hard as iron. I cut the dandelions as close to the ground as possible, getting the thick base where the serrated leaves join the roots and the texture is more like that of a starchy vegetable than a leafy green; this also helps hold the leaves together. I cut off the tops, which were too green and bitter for my taste, and ended up with rosettes about 2 inches long. Thirty of these were easily enough, my bag was half full and my bones were cold. I headed home to make hot chocolate and decide what to cook for dinner.

Spelt risotto with roasted winter veg and dandelion rosettes

Dandelions are extremely versatile, with edible leaves, roots and flowers. If you like bitter greens, which I know many people do, try the leaves in a salad instead of chicory or wilted with parmesan and a splash of olive oil. Their hollow stems don't make good eating but even these, with a little imagination, can become straws through which to drink wild cocktails.

1 sweet potato, 2 onions, 1 courgette, 1 red pepper, 6 garlic cloves, sprigs of mugwort (or rosemary and thyme), rapeseed oil, 6 cherry tomatoes, 200g pearled spelt, 80ml white wine (give or take the odd sip), 1 litre vegetable stock, a dozen or so dandelion rosettes, grated parmesan, salt and pepper

Serves 4

Preheat the oven to 200°C/gas 6. Chop the sweet potato, one of the onions, the courgette and the red pepper into 2cm cubes or thick slices. Put them in a baking dish with the garlic and herbs, pour over the oil to cover and season with some salt and pepper. Bake for about 25 minutes, adding the cherry tomatoes for the last 5 minutes and roasting until they burst.

For the risotto, finely chop the other onion and fry it slowly in a generous amount of oil before adding the pearled spelt and stirring for a few seconds. Add the white wine and simmer until all the liquid has been absorbed. Now add all the stock (yes, all), season with salt and pepper and add the dandelion rosettes. Simmer for about 25 minutes, stirring occasionally until all the liquid has been absorbed, then add the roasted vegetables and serve with lots of parmesan.

For a tasty side dish, cook any spare rosettes in a little water or stock until the bases are tender.

COW PARSLEY
Anthriscus sylvestris

Umbrella-shaped flowers made up of smaller flowers (called compound umbels) with five irregular petals on each

Leaves dividing into many lobed leaflets. Divisions and leaflets shorter nearer the tip

Grows 60–100cm tall and has a fresh herby smell when broken

PARTS USED: Leaves, stems, flowers, seeds

HARVESTING TIP: Do not confuse with deadly poisonous hemlock (*Conium maculatum*) or other poisonous lookalikes. For more information read the section on page 267

8th January. Ravenscourt Park

This afternoon, while hurrying through a beautiful little park in the west of the city, I was presented with a vast carpet of young green tufts of cow parsley, aka wild chervil, one of my favourite and most utilized wild foods. With feathery green carrot-top leaves, cow parsley is annually the first of the Carrot family to put up new growth and has a second flush in early autumn. It's also the first to flower in the spring, with distinct white umbrella flowers (umbels). I serve the leaves as a salad until they get too tough (usually in late spring), when I start using them as a cooked green, after which I start eating the young stems, then the flowers, then the seeds; it's such a versatile plant. I was in a rush today, so in traditional hunter-gatherer style, I picked and ran – I always keep a cloth bag on me for missions like this – and within literally a minute I had enough greenery to last me for a week.

I can't overstress the need for caution when looking at plants in the Carrot family, where the delicious and the deadly meet; this is not a place for experimentation. On the one hand we have extremely poisonous plants like hemlock, hemlock water dropwort and the garden-loving fool's parsley, while on the other, we have fennel, dill, coriander, wild carrot, hogweed and many other tasty wild and domestic plants. A tricky and dangerous place for the novice forager to spend any time, but it's vital to know what they look like, if for no other reason than to avoid them. My advice: go on an organized walk with someone very experienced and get them to show you first-hand what is and what isn't edible and how to tell them apart. When running my own foraging walks, I teach people how to 'crush and sniff' their way to safety by hard wiring the smell of cow parsley, but the responses I get when I ask people to describe it include everything from lemons and pears, carrot and parsley, to washing powder or varnish and the classic lazy answer, 'It just smells green.' My favourite response was, 'It smells of hippies!' But however this plant smells, good or bad, it DOES NOT smell like hemlock, the most likely poisonous plant to confuse it with. This, above all else, is the bit of information that we can use to keep us out of harm's way, but, as I hope I have made abundantly clear, it smells very differently to everyone . . . so you'll just need to go on a guided foraging walk and find out for yourself.

The mighty wild green smoothie

500ml good-quality apple juice (or a mix of juice and water if you prefer), 3–4 handfuls of green leaves, wild ones and/or spinach, chard, etc., ½ avocado, juice of 1 lemon, 2.5cm lump of ginger root, 1 garlic clove (optional if drinking first thing in the morning), a big pinch of turmeric, some chilli or cayenne (or honey)

Serves 1

I can't stand reading anything too smugly self-righteous, especially about healthy eating, so please don't think for a second that I don't totally overindulge over Christmas – the only wild food I consume is thoroughly soaked in booze. Like most people, come the really chilly months I don't tend to fancy a salad, but because I habitually pick wild plants, which are young and tender at this time of year, I find a brilliant way to use them and also get my fix of vitamins, minerals, nutrients and a host of other goodies, is to make smoothies, with part wild and part shop-bought ingredients. A daily drink like this will also help cleanse the liver and boost the immune system. As a smoothie ingredient, young cow parsley gives a great flavour but it's not vital and unless 100 per cent sure of your identification, substitute the cow parsley with some domestic parsley, dill or chervil. Amongst other wild greens, I added some yarrow, chickweed, dandelion, winter cress, hedge mustard and cleavers, aka sticky weed. The recipe is simple, so adjust the quantities depending on how much you want to drink (half a litre is plenty) and the ingredients based on what you have to hand.

Blend the apple juice (or a mix of juice and water) with the green leaves, avocado, lemon juice, ginger and garlic. Stir in the turmeric and, if you fancy, a little chilli or cayenne. To go in a sweeter direction you could add honey instead of the last two spices. I promise that once you get into making these drinks it becomes a very enjoyable daily ritual.

WINTER CRESS

Barbarea vulgaris

Many flowering stems with
tiny yellow flowers and
broccoli-like buds at the tip

Smooth and shiny leaves
with a large terminal
leaflet and lobes that vary
in shape

PARTS USED: Leaves, seeds

HARVESTING TIP: Avoid possibly polluted spots such as
tree bases and roadsides where this plant often flourishes

15th January. At home

It's cold, it's wet and it's almost dark by 3 p.m. . . . This is England, in mid-January. Strangely enough, I love this time of year in the city; as always, there is plenty of wild food about, but it's certainly a quieter time on the foraging calendar and this creates all manner of opportunities, indoors as well as out. The cyclical nature of the plants I collect means there is never a gap, in fact there are so many overlaps, it's impossible to ever really just stop and take stock. The darkest of winter days, when leaving the house seems like a horrific chore, provides a great chance to do some catching up. My ever-increasing pile of books gets fractionally reduced, lots of the autumn fruits, hastily picked and chucked in the freezer, find their way into all manner of syrups, cordials and sauces, plans for the spring begin to form, ideas for new events and new walks take shape. In many ways my spring starts here, in the depths of winter.

Having escaped the house, I bought a hot chocolate, and in the communal gardens a couple of minutes from my house, found a patch of dark green winter cress, a land-growing relative of watercress sometimes called yellow rocket, which looks vaguely similar to the rocket you'll recognize from supermarket salad bags, but with thick shiny leaves. The big question is, what to put with it on such a chilly and brooding day as this, and the answer lies in only one place, the bottom of the freezer! It fascinates me how perfectly the ancient and fundamental tasks of gathering, preparing and storing food dovetail so well into various bits of modern technology, and I can think of no greater tool for the contemporary hunter-gatherer than a decent freezer. This ability to so effectively preserve numerous different foods, without the addition of masses of sugar or lengthy processes like curing and smoking, gives us a way of extending the use of many of our wild and non-wild foods that our ancestors would have considered magical. So what is it that lay at the bottom of this chilly treasure chest? Hidden beneath a huge bag of rose hips lurked the last of the previous season's wild garlic, aka ransoms, which I'd sweated, bagged and frozen into portions that never normally make it through the year, let alone into the beginning of the next. If the weather was kind to us, this wonderful, all-purpose wild food would be popping its head up in just a few weeks' time, months ahead of some other parts of the country. For now I was very happy with the small amount I had and set about the task of reviving it and doing it justice.

Winter cress, wild garlic and chorizo soup

6 big handfuls of winter cress, 6 big handfuls of wild garlic, 2–3 tbsp of oil, 1 litre good chicken or vegetable stock, soy sauce, black pepper, 1 potato (optional), a 10cm piece of chorizo, 1 onion, 1 tsp mustard seeds, 1–2 tsp brown sugar, ¼–1 tsp celery salt

Serves 4–6

Invented, like so many of my recipes, by using what came to hand, this truly is a delicious and simple thing to prepare. Half winter cress and half wild garlic (for more on wild garlic see page 43), although the latter of these came from the freezer; ideally I'd prefer to use fresh leaves and stems, or those of its close relative three-cornered leek, which I find in season in the city from around October right through into the spring.

I'd recommend about half a carrier bag of greenery, washed and then sweated with a splash of oil for a few minutes to reduce. Now whizz it in a blender for just a few seconds (or use a mouli later on, once the soup is cooked). In a heavy pan, add the greens to the stock with a decent slug of soy sauce and some black pepper, also a cubed potato if you want something a bit thicker. Cook this slowly for half an hour and while that's happening cut the chorizo into 1cm cubes and fry on its own for a minute or two to release lots of the oil. I discard this oil but it's up to you. Set the chorizo aside then slowly fry a diced onion with the mustard seeds until soft, then add the brown sugar and carry on at a very low heat

25th January. Esher, south-west of London, just

'Which species of crab apple is this?' the man asked me as I was carefully removing its fruits. 'Not a clue,' I replied. With hundreds of varieties, it's not the species, subspecies or cultivar that's relevant, it's the taste, and this can vary widely from tree to tree, as can the size, the number of fruits and the best time to pick them. But there we were, in the suburbs in mid-winter, and this tree still had plenty of fruit on it – small bunches of juicy yellow ovals flushed with rosy pink patches. Unlike most of 'my' central London crab apple trees, which were fully fruiting and ready to pick by 1 September. Fortunately, with only this one to choose from, the little apples all over it tasted fantastic, slightly tart but still very sweet. As for the rest of my surroundings, they seemed pretty barren at first glance, a patch of grassy common land, surrounded by bare trees and some scrubby woodland. Only on closer examination did it reveal all manner of young green salad plants starting to come through: sow thistle, nipplewort, yarrow, clover, dandelion and very young garlic mustard, flushed with a delicate kale-like purple.

Then in my peripheral vision, a flash of bright orange that my brain couldn't quite compute, a huge scraggly bush, covered with massive spines; maybe not looking for a fight but certainly ready for one. Sea buckthorn! This wild and wonderfully aggressive-looking coastal shrub was a long way from home, growing here on the outskirts of the city and doing extremely well, too. Removing the easily exploding clusters of intensely flavoured orange berries is a real skill and a steady hand is useful in avoiding its huge spines. Although now somewhat redundant, they were evolved to repel much larger predators than me. If you've never tried sea buckthorn, imagine a turbo-charged version of orange meets lemon with the intensity dial set to maximum, generally a real shock to first-timers. Half an hour later I had enough berries to add to my crab apples, both brightly coloured and both reminiscent of those lovely sharp sweets – sours, I think they are called. At home I set about creating my own version. Although lacking the sugar of all those Christmas chocolates and cakes, these would still be just as tasty and give me something sweet, but much healthier, to get me through the chilly weeks ahead.

Crab apple fruit chews with sea buckthorn and star anise

500g crab apples, 3–4 handfuls of sea buckthorn berries, 2 star anise, 1 cinnamon stick (optional), sugar or xylitol fruit sugar, ½ banana (optional)

Traditionally referred to as fruit leathers – not a title I like – these amazing fruit sweets are simple to make, need no added sugar and keep, in the freezer if needed, for absolutely ages. Combine both these extreme fruits and you have some truly amazing nibbles.

Chop your crab apples and mix with the sea buckthorn berries, adding ½ cup of water for every 4 cups of fruit. Add the star anise, the cinnamon too if you fancy, and simmer it all for about 20 minutes until soft, before giving the mix a good squash with a potato masher. At this point you could add some sugar to taste or a fruit sugar like xylitol or, better still, no sugar at all.

Carry on cooking for another 10 minutes or so before removing the anise and cinnamon and putting it all into a blender. The aim is to get a smooth paste, so if you find the mix is too thin, blend in half a banana to help it stiffen slightly.

Lastly, the mixture needs to be smeared, no thicker than 2–3 mm, onto sheets of lightly greased baking paper and dried in a very low oven for 8–10 hours, unless you are lucky enough to have a dehydrator, in which case it takes less time and uses a lot less power.

Remove the finished chews from their paper, cut them into strips and store in a tin. Alternatively, fold up each sheet of paper with the dried mixture still on it and put it in the freezer. Needless to say this recipe works well with all manner of fruit, whether wild, domestic or a mix of both.

SEA BUCKTHORN
Elaeagnus rhamnoides

Long narrow leaves
with rounded tips

Many bright orange
berries attached all
along the branches

Long sharp thorns

PARTS USED: Fruit

HARVESTING TIP: Watch out for
those thorns and the exploding berries

JAPANESE MAHONIA

Berberis japonica

Long clusters of small yellow
flowers extending outwards
from the centre of the leaves

Sharp holly-like leaves

Small, dark purple,
grape-like berries

PARTS USED: Flowers, fruit

HARVESTING TIP: Timing is everything; on the right day the flowers taste
sweet or sharp like grapefruit, on the wrong day they are quite bitter

30th January. Shoreditch

A capital city is nothing if not varied; a blend of strange ingredients, a social, cultural, architectural and ecological hotchpotch: ideal for the urban forager wanting to experience the unusual and experiment with new flavours, textures and ideas. Today, I had a meeting with the council, lunch with a media-obsessed friend and a visit to a firm of architects who wanted to organize a wild food walk. Surrounded by skyscrapers, congested roads and swarms of commuters, it was hard, even for me, to be in foraging mode. On my way home, walking along Kingsland Road, I found myself leaving a Vietnamese grocer's with a dozen sheets of dried rice paper. Did I really need these? What was I going to do with them? What would a Vietnamese urban forager do right now? I headed for the nearest patch of greenery, Shoreditch Park, an odd little spot, mostly just grass and a massive boulder plonked right in the middle, as if Hanuman himself had dropped it there. I wasn't expecting much, but noticed two large mounds at the far side, a few hundred yards from the road. Further investigation revealed some interesting 'guerrilla' planting, a semi-wild area, a haven for numerous tasty edible plants, most of which are only very small at this time of year. Ring-fenced to keep out kids, dogs and any other urban invaders, a delicate touch would be necessary here, but I really only needed a few leaves of each, so that's all I took.

Before leaving I picked a few flowers from a nearby Japanese mahonia, a bush that's planted in almost every London park as a robust hedge. I often find the closely related Oregon grape, too. Both these species resemble stocky little holly bushes with sharp evergreen leaves, big spikes or bunches of yellow flowers in the winter and edible purple 'grapes' in the summer. As a salad these flowers are best around early December when they are sweet with a grapefruit tang, but cooked or in smoothies they are useful and attractive whenever you find them. Inspired by my multicultural impulse purchase, it was off home to do some wrapping.

Spring rolls with Japanese mahonia flowers and wild salad leaves

With their sharp citrus flavour, I love to use mahonia flowers in wild sushi and later in the year to make a wine from their ripe purple berries, which I also include in jellies and fruit leathers (try adapting the crab apple and sea buckthorn recipe on page 24 if you fancy having a go at this).

For the rolls: rice paper, rice wine vinegar (optional), mahonia flowers, red chilli, grated carrot, (whatever you have in the fridge that's crunchy and fresh)

For the dipping sauce: 4 tbsp soy sauce, 2 tbsp sesame oil, 2 tbsp thin honey

This isn't really a recipe, more a guide to assemblage, but before you begin, the dried rice paper needs a quick dip in some tepid water, about a minute, until it's slightly sticky, then patting dry on paper towels. At this stage you could also drizzle on some rice wine vinegar to give the finished rolls an extra piquant tang. In warmer weather I lay my flowers and salads across the sheet and roll them, not too tightly, the last edge sticking it all together, then without cooking them, serve whole or cut into smaller sections with as sharp a knife as possible. More appropriate for a cold day is to go for a tighter roll, folding in the ends like a burrito and dropping the whole parcel into a pan of hot oil for 2–3 minutes . . . hey presto, wild spring rolls!

For the dipping sauce I use a mix of soy, sesame oil and thin honey but obviously you can use any condiment you fancy, home-made or otherwise (Thai sweet chilli sauce is always a winner). I often mix and match wild and bought ingredients when making these rolls, sometimes adding finely chopped cabbage or broccoli, bean sprouts, or whatever comes to hand. This is such a great food to assemble with a group, either as a hot dish on a chilly day or as picnic food when the weather warms up.

February

Nettle and three-cornered leek gnocchi

A seasonal chickweed salad with very early
spring leaves and flowers

Cold-crushing super soup, aka Satan's own chilli soup

Wild garlic, goat's cheese and caramelized onion tart

Garlic mustard omelette and fried green sprinkles

*'There they were, nestled in a slightly damp and shady corner of
the park, with delicious new shoots and leaves about 3 inches
high, popping up to see what the spring would bring . . .'*

THREE-CORNERED LEEK
Allium triquetrum

Six white petals, each
with a green stripe
down the centre

Flowering stems
are triangular in
cross-section

Narrow leaves,
12–20cm long

PARTS USED: Leaves, flowers, stems, bulbs, seeds

HARVESTING TIP: Has a very long season
running from October–May

2nd February. A nature reserve, hiding between Highbury and Holloway

Bloody hell, it's cold! My friend Adam is from Canada and back home they regularly get temperatures as low as minus 25 in the winter, but as he is fond of telling me, 'It's just cold, not this crappy, soul-destroying, *damp* cold that you get in the UK.'

Today the weather was exactly as he describes it, but having been at home far too much lately I headed to one of my most loved foraging spots, a tiny park-cum-nature reserve, just a few minutes from my house. The trees were bare and the ground hard, but the path edges and grassland were looking very promising. Ahead of me was a sea of alexanders, a wild member of the Carrot family, introduced into the UK by the Romans, and although traditionally a coastal plant, thriving here in the city and putting up fat green stems and lush bluey-green foliage. Unlike some, I'm not a huge fan of this plant. It's similar to angelica, with a perfumed smell and flavour, but its dried seeds in mid-summer do make an excellent stand-in for black pepper and would have been popular as a spice hundreds of years before the spice trade brought the more exotic equivalents to our shores.

Today, however, my attentions were focused on two other plants: stinging nettles (which we'll encounter in more detail in April) and a wonderful 'invasive' relative of garlic called three-cornered leek. The nettles are only tiny at this time of year but the top couple of inches or so were a lovely shiny green, snapping at just the right point, the plant letting me know which bit to pick and which to leave behind. I pretty much smelt the 'leeks' before I saw them and, as with so many of the plants I forage for, they crept into my peripheral vision before I realized I was utterly surrounded by them. At first glance, an early patch of three-cornered leek can look a bit like long, thick grass, but on closer examination it's easy to see where this delicious plant gets its name, the flower stems having three distinct corners to them – and of course that wonderful garlic meets leek meets onion smell.

Nettle and three-cornered leek gnocchi

Alternative uses for both of these abound and some can be found in later pages. Think nettle pesto (instead of traditional basil), three-cornered leek hummus (just tweak my recipe for rocket hummus on page 130) or an omelette with leaves from both plants folded into the centre. These two ingredients could just as easily have become the base of a great soup but I fancied something with a bit more 'stodge'.

500g waxy potatoes, 50g grated parmesan plus extra to serve, a good fistful each of finely chopped nettles and three-cornered leeks, 200g plain flour plus extra for dusting, olive oil, salt and pepper

Serves 4–6

First peel and boil the spuds, drain, and mash them thoroughly before adding generous amounts of salt and black pepper, then the parmesan and the nettles and three-cornered leeks (spinach is a good stand-in if it's too early in the year to pick nettles). At this point you could whizz the whole lot in a blender or food processor, but I don't bother. Next add the plain flour; amounts will vary so add it gradually, mixing with your hands until you get a dough that's not too dense but holds together well enough to roll into little balls. Roll out long sausages of the dough on a flour-dusted surface and chop them through every 2.5cm to make your individual gnocchlettes (OK, I'll admit I made that word up).

Now drop one into a large pan of boiling water and cook until it floats to the surface (a couple of minutes). Use this one as a test for the others; you may want them cooked for a bit longer and so they'll need to stay in the water for 10 or 20 seconds after they surface. Cook the whole batch and serve with oil, salt and parmesan to really get the flavour of the plants, or a tomato and chilli sauce for a heartier dish.

CHICKWEED
Stellaria media

Tiny flowers
with five petals
that split deeply
down the centre

A line of white hairs
runs along one side of
the rounded stems

Leaves almost oval, though
wider at the base and in
opposite pairs on the stems

PARTS USED: Leaves, flowers, young stems

HARVESTING TIP: Snip off the top of large bunches with scissors to allow for regrowth

8th February. Battersea Park

Despite the almost freezing weather, plenty of the salad plants that thrive in the city were busy getting ready for spring, some behaving like it was here already. A salad may seem the most unlikely of mid-winter meals but I try to eat plenty of wild greens all year round. As any busy urbanite will tell you, the recipe with the least effort is very often the one most likely to get made. The cold weather may lend itself more to a hearty soup or stew but the combined nutritional value and health-giving properties of the dozen or so ingredients I'd normally use in a wild salad will go toe to toe with any winter hotpot. With vitamins B and C, beta-carotene, magnesium, zinc, calcium, antioxidants, protein and fibre, and the amazing array of wild flavours, it puts the tasteless shop-bought lettuce, spinach and, worst of all, mono-flavoured 'salad mix' that comes in a bag full of farty gas, totally to shame.

Battersea Park has many of the things I look for in an urban green space, a mix of managed and unmanaged areas, interesting tree planting, some water's edge and a smattering of woodland – basically a variety of varied and overlapping environments, making an ideal location to hunt for free, healthy food. Today was no exception and I ended up in the park having made the commitment to leave the warmth of the bus I was on as it travelled over Battersea Bridge, the view from on high and the lure of the outdoors was just too strong. Ten minutes later I had what I came for, basically a wild mixed salad: a fine selection of crow garlic shoots, ox-eye daisy leaves, feathery fennel shoots, hairy bittercress, yarrow leaves and some very early primrose flowers, not really wild but growing randomly at the edge of the park – I tend to think of them as feral. My main ingredient came from a big bunch of chickweed that I'd carefully extracted from the middle of an ornamental flower bed. With tiny white petals and rambling pale green foliage, this low-growing plant is a great winter staple, crunchy and sweet with a hint of pea to its flavour. I headed back to the bus stop, re-entering the metropolis, jostling with everyone else in the street, but with my small cloth bag full of wild leaves, perhaps feeling just a little calmer than they were, for the time being at least.

A seasonal chickweed salad with very early spring leaves and flowers

Chickweed, ox-eye daisy, hairy bittercress, crow garlic, yarrow, primrose flowers, fennel, sweet vinegar, olive oil, salt and black pepper

As the instructions for this salad are basically: stick all the wild ingredients in a bowl, cover in a vinaigrette dressing, I've got time to tell you a bit more about these wonderful plants.

Chickweed is a great 'base' ingredient for a wild salad, with a sweet and pleasant taste; it's simple to ID, with only the slightly similar scarlet pimpernel likely to confuse the novice forager. And it's very easy to gather a big bunch in just a few seconds, although never from the base of a London tree, where it tends to thrive due to the generous donation of nitrogen found in dog wee. Use your common sense and forage out of and away from the dog-wee zone.

The other ingredients in my salad included ox-eye daisy, a terrific and unusual-tasting salad plant. I munch its leaves all year round and the yellow and white flowers are delicious, too. In fact, following the recipe for nettle leaves on page 111, they also make a great tempura. Hairy bittercress, not really hairy or bitter, is a lovely peppery member of the cabbage family, often found growing in outdoor pot plants. Try it roughly chopped over scrambled eggs or if you're feeling fancy, use a few sprigs to decorate the top of some pan-fried salmon.

Crow garlic – actually this was probably domestic chives but let's stick with the wild name; everyone knows how this tastes. Washed and finely chopped, it makes a perfect topping for boiled and mashed potatoes. All the edible members of this family are vital in a good winter diet, keeping colds at bay and lowering cholesterol.

Yarrow, with feathery leaves and a distinctive savoury flavour, is also good in teas and as a pot herb later in the season. It's a great 'bitter herb', encouraging good digestion, acting as a diuretic and helping to purify the blood. The primrose flowers definitely weren't wild, so should probably be called primula. The leaves were bitter and tough, unlike the beautiful subtle wild version; the flowers, however, were sweet, delicate and great to add some colour.

Fennel, not the big bulbed variety but the tall and feathery version, a fruity and fragrant member of the Carrot family, has an aniseed flavour which works brilliantly with fish . . . actually it's great with everything (more info on page 93). This was a very young shoot but easy to spot next to last year's dead stalks with their umbrella-shaped seed heads still intact. Only for the more experienced forager, so beware dangerous lookalikes (we'll cover this in more detail later on).

A sweet vinegar will help to bring together all the flavours of a wild salad, taking the edge off the bitter ones and enhancing the more fragrant, so I usually use a home-made wild rose vinegar (recipe on page 198) and plenty of olive or rapeseed oil.

HORSERADISH

Armoracia rusticana

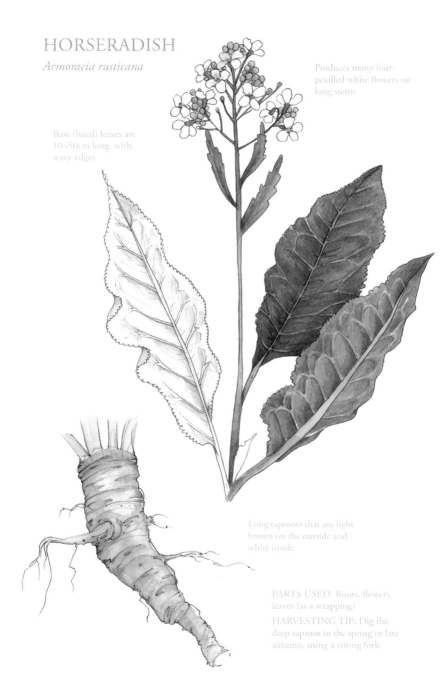

Produces many four-petalled white flowers on long stems

Base (basal) leaves are 10–50cm long, with wavy edges

Long taproots that are light brown on the outside and white inside

PARTS USED: Roots, flowers, leaves (as a wrapping)

HARVESTING TIP: Dig the deep taproot in the spring or late autumn, using a strong fork

13th February. At home

I do not get colds, I do not get colds, I DO NOT GET COLDS.
Actually, truth be told, I still rarely get a bad one but since the arrival
of my son, 'the conduit for all the germs in London', as I sometimes
call him, I do tend to get the odd sniffle. As I have a strong immune
system, bolstered with years of munching on nutrient-rich wild plants,
they never progress into anything worse than a day on the settee and an
opportunity to catch up on some reading or, at very worst, the guiltiest
of pleasures, daytime TV.

My basic rule of thumb is to cook with spices, as many of them as
possible, all winter long. Without doubt, my most powerful combatant of
any winter cold is this Super Spicy Blow Your Head Clean Off Immune-
Boosting Soup. It contains masses of turmeric; the numerous documented
medicinal properties of this plant are extraordinary. Here are just a few:
anti-inflammatory, antibiotic, antiseptic, analgesic (pain-killing), purifies
the blood and lowers cholesterol. Furthermore, turmeric has been used
in treatments for asthma, arthritis, MS, eczema, psoriasis, to boost the
immune system during chemotherapy and to slow the progression of
Alzheimer's. What a wonderful spice; it's easily available and it can be
incorporated into almost all winter cooking. Add to this some garlic,
capable of converting 'bad' cholesterol (LDL) into 'good' cholesterol
(HDL), reducing blood pressure and stabilizing blood sugar levels as well
as being a natural antibiotic, antiseptic and expectorant (helping to thin
and clear mucus). And fresh or powdered chilli to help purify the blood
and boost the circulation. The alkaloid capsaicin, which gives chillies that
characteristic strong, spicy flavour, has been shown in laboratory studies
to be anti-bacterial, analgesic and anti-diabetic. Next we have ginger, a
plant described as 'the world's healthiest food', fantastic cut into chunks
and used as a tea, well known for its calming effects on the stomach, as an
immune booster and as a treatment for nausea.

The one wild ingredient I collected for my soup was horseradish.
I say wild but that's really stretching the truth: I didn't plant it but a

small patch appeared a few months ago in my tiny back garden. Going outside today to dig up the roots of this wonderfully pungent relative of rocket and mustard was as far from home as I got. It's a very easy plant to recognize with a distinct fishbone pattern to its upright and pointed, dark green leaves. If in any doubt, crush one and give it a sniff. Horseradish sauce? Bingo.

Cold-crushing super soup, aka Satan's own chilli soup

If you're lucky enough to have a good supply of horseradish you might consider using its leaves to wrap around fish while they bake or thinly slicing and deep-frying the roots to make horseradish crisps. For a traditional sauce, blend grated horseradish root with a little white wine vinegar, salt and mustard powder, adding double cream or crème fraiche. Roast beef aside, this sauce is perfect for bringing a bit of zing to almost any meal and nothing beats a couple of spoonfuls mixed into mashed potato.

24 garlic cloves, 4–6 red chillies, 10–15cm of horseradish root, 5–10cm of fresh root ginger, 1–2 tbsp of chopped turmeric root (or 2–4 tsp ground), 3 tsp of cayenne, 3 tsp of black pepper, half a litre vegetable stock, soy sauce, tomato purée

Serves 1–2 brave people

It was nutritionist supremo Lorna Driver-Davies who first introduced me to this soup. Not a wild remedy but no cold can stand in its way and if prepared properly it should be almost more pain than pleasure. I make the 'base' ingredients of mine into frozen cubes to use quickly when I really need it. Stuffed to the gills with immune-boosting turmeric, expectorant garlic, antioxidant-rich horseradish and blood-purifying chilli, I find it most effective when shouting 'OUT DEMONS OUT' between mouthfuls – not a compulsory act but it can help distract you from the other effects. I don't usually do 'health and safety' but this soup is probably not for anyone with a dodgy ticker.

And the recipe (the quantities on the previous page are what I use but can be adjusted according to taste) . . . Fry copious amounts (just keep chopping until you can't chop any more) of garlic, chilli, horseradish, ginger and turmeric root (powder is fine), then add far too much cayenne and black pepper, stock, soy sauce and tomato purée. The end result is a hugely over-spiced thick soup – don't use too much liquid, you want to get this inside you as quickly as possible and if it's almost too horrid to eat you have done well . . . Mix it with a bit of tinned soup to make it more bearable, if you must, or use it as a base for a gentler version by adding another litre of stock, vegetables, lime juice and a splash of fish sauce. I once delivered a batch of this powerful medicine to my friend Gav. In his own words, 'I went from feeling like I was breathing through two hedgehogs instead of lungs – all the extra-strength cold and flu remedies doing absolutely nothing to relieve this – to feeling not that bad in just three hours. Half an hour after ingesting it, my head began to boil and I then spent an hour or so with a high fever. I woke up to find that my illness had been reduced to a mild headache with some slight aching, but no mucus whatsoever.' So there you have it.

WILD GARLIC
Allium ursinum

Six-petalled
white flowers

Seeds each
made of three
green balls

Long broad leaves

Individual bulbs with roots
at the base of the leaf stalk

PARTS USED: Leaves, stems, flowers, bulbs, seeds

HARVESTING TIP: Don't get carried away picking and always
check carefully for toxic plants that grow in amongst the leaves

25th February. A nature reserve south of the river

My city is full of free gifts; pretty much every day I win a prize without ever entering a competition. It's not really about free food, or even the diversity of tastes and textures and the opportunities these present, it's the places where I find all my treasures, pockets of the city that seem invisible to almost everyone else. Although the media would have us believe that foraging is some sort of fad – which is of course a ludicrous way to describe how mankind has fed itself from the dawn of our existence until very recently. The number of people I actually meet with a similar purpose to mine is almost none, even at the height of the mushroom-picking season in the autumn, when far from being swamped with greedy wild food enthusiasts, the woods I visit are deserted. Last week I had a call from an ecology centre asking if I'd like to host some events for them. It's always lovely to hear from people who totally get the concept of wild food in the city rather than feeling threatened by the idea of encouraging people to look for food outside of their local supermarket (oops, politics, sorry). Paying them a visit today, the sun was out and I was able to kill two birds with the same stone, finally getting a ride on the cable car that crosses the Thames between Greenwich and Canning Town. From on high I had amazing views of the city, the river winding and widening as it heads east, the huge towers of Canary Wharf, the financial district to the west and the world-famous Royal Observatory sitting in the middle of Greenwich Park to the east. And, most importantly to me, despite this central location, numerous open and green spaces.

The park itself was small but with very diverse plant life, reed beds, grasslands and patches of birch trees and coppiced hazel. Best of all, very early indeed, a wide patch of ransoms, otherwise known as wild garlic. There they were, nestled in a slightly damp and shady corner of the park, with delicious new shoots and leaves about 3 inches high, popping up to see what the spring would bring. I collected enough to fill both pockets of my winter coat (it does have very big pockets).

Wild garlic, goat's cheese and caramelized onion tart

Wild garlic is a firm favourite with foragers and for good reason: it produces five edible crops: leaves, stems, bulbs, flowers and seeds. The last of these need collecting while they are still green, plucked from the top of the stems just after the flowers drop, and they make the most amazing wild garlic 'capers'. It's a simple process but one that involves gathering hundreds of seeds, sprinkling them with salt, then leaving them for a couple of weeks before pickling in a mild vinegar (cider or white wine). The only problem I have with these wonderful little bombs of flavour is when it comes to sharing them! It's worth mentioning that there are a few toxic plants that grow with wild garlic, most notably bluebells and lords and ladies, both of which have a similar green colour but very different-shaped foliage. Be extra careful to avoid any confusion if digging up the bulbs.

2 large red onions, olive oil, balsamic vinegar, 2–3 tbsp brown sugar, 4 sheets of filo pastry, 6 x 100g wheels of goat's cheese, 2 large handfuls of chopped wild garlic leaves and stems

Serves 6

I would love to take the credit for this recipe but instead I will just have to bask in reflected glory. I had planned nothing more elaborate for my wild garlic than a couple of minutes in the steamer, but when I emptied my pockets onto our kitchen table, my wife Ellie had other plans; she paused, looked pensive and five seconds later I could see the light bulb go on. What I love most about this recipe is that it takes four individually gorgeous flavours and allows them to effortlessly coexist without detracting from them.

First the caramelized onion, made by roughly chopping the onions and frying very gently in oil for 10 minutes before adding a few generous slugs of balsamic vinegar and the brown sugar, then cooking slowly for another 15 minutes or so.

For the tart itself, grease a decent-sized baking dish then line with the sheets of filo pastry and arrange the wheels of goat's cheese on top, covering them with the chopped wild garlic leaves and stems and topping off with the caramelized onion mix. Bake in a low to medium oven for 25 minutes. I could eat this every day until I become too large to leave the house.

GARLIC MUSTARD
Alliara petiolata

Clusters of small four-petalled white flowers

The more mature, upper leaves are far more complex than the younger ones

The young leaves are roughly heart-shaped with a smooth, slightly waxy texture on top

Leaves, when broken, smell garlicky and mustardy

PARTS USED: Leaves, flowers, seeds, roots
HARVESTING TIP: Start picking as early as January and remember the flavour gets stronger and stronger as the year goes on

28th February. A playground in Finsbury Park

Springtime. It's such an evocative word, imbued with a warm glow and the hope of better weather, more time spent outdoors and the shedding of all those cumbersome winter layers. Today I could see signs of its arrival waving at me from all over the park: hawthorn trees with their first, nutty-flavoured young leaves, cherry plum already covered in pale pink blossoms, linden trees producing thousands of tiny bright red buds, which in another month or so will open into heart-shaped leaves but for now were wrapped up tight. The sun was out, low in the sky and much needed, but Finsbury Park can be very windy and my wardrobe mirrored the weather – sunglasses and a thick coat, dressed for the cusp of two seasons and, just like the trees, the other plants and everyone else in the city, desperate for spring to do its thing. Unlike me, my son does not feel the cold; I am unsure he even knows that the concept exists and he was blissfully happy, sitting in the middle of a large sandpit, chilly air whipping around us, lost in a noisy dialogue with his toys. My attention wandered and I shuffled my feet to stay warm, then another child, a friend from nursery, with his mother, came to my aid, and before I knew it, I'd delivered the classic parental request: 'Do you mind keeping your eye on him for a few minutes?'

Coffee drinking and speed foraging, I have both of these down to a fine art and sometimes my window of opportunity only opens just enough for me to grab whatever comes to hand – perhaps a truer reflection of traditional hunting and gathering than the times when I can be more selective. A quick scan of a nearby flower bed, ideal for urban foraging with recently turned soil and a protective border of wooden stakes: cow parsley, young nettles (always good news for me) and a lovely patch of garlic mustard, light green but with the tinge of purple you'd find on a good kale. This delicious member of the cabbage family does a great impression of garlic, if not visually then certainly in the way it smells and tastes.

I felt an omelette coming on . . . 'Oscar, it's home time.'

Garlic mustard omelette and fried green sprinkles

At this time of year, garlic mustard produces just two heart-shaped leaves, often not much bigger than a couple of inches across, simple and with a gently wavy edge. As the year goes on, not only does its appearance change, the plant getting much taller, the leaves more complex, but the flavour shifts from a gentle garlic to an intensely strong version of itself, often with a bitter aftertaste, still great for using in soups and stews but far too strong for much else, certainly not a salad plant. Also known as Jack-by-the-hedge or hedge garlic, this is the perfect time of year for me to use this power-packed little plant. Some people enjoy the taste of raw garlic mustard leaves but they're usually too intense for my palate unless they've been cooked, definitely becoming too bitter as the year progresses. You might try using the bigger leaves instead of nettles in my tempura recipe on page 111, or the wonderful white flowers that it produces in the late spring will give a spicy kick when added to any salad.

For the omelette: 4 eggs, milk, chopped nettle and garlic mustard leaves, salt and pepper

For the sprinkles: finely chopped cow parsley, nettle and garlic mustard leaves. A handful of each is plenty

Serves 2

For our lunch I made a four-egg omelette with chopped-up nettle and garlic mustard leaves. The nettle ceases to be a stinger once it's cooked but, to be sure, I dropped mine into boiling water for 30 seconds before I added them with the garlic mustard leaves to the beaten egg and milk mixture. Nettles are wonderful at this time of year, just the very youngest growth available, a bright happy green, packed with protein, iron and silica.

To create my own urban version of furikake, a marvellous Japanese condiment made from dried seaweed and sesame, I washed, chopped and dry-fried (almost no oil) a mix of cow parsley, nettle and garlic mustard leaves, just until they all became crispy, then crushed them with my hands and sprinkled them all over our omelettes. This is an excellent way to create a healthy flavour enhancer for numerous dishes, either spread over the top or mixed in as an ingredient and will work with all sorts of wild and not so wild greens as long as they are quite tender and will dry-fry quickly.

March

Ground ivy and wild garlic pakoras

Winter purslane pesto and numerous other ideas

Steamed and fried hogweed shoots

Burdock root 'four ways'

Sea beet cooked with secret ingredients

'These unfurled shoots were all between 3 and 4 inches high,
the perfect time to pick them, and currently presenting only
one danger to the unprepared forager, nestled as they were
among thousands of very young stinging nettles . . .'

GROUND IVY
Glechoma hederacea

Square stems with opposite pairs of
leaves – each pair is at right angles
to the pair above and below

Heart- to kidney-shaped
leaves with rounded teeth.
Creeping growth

Pale blue to violet flowers

PARTS USED: Leaves, flowers

HARVESTING TIP: Easier to harvest when flowering
but once you know the smell it is simple to identify

3rd March. A secret location somewhere in London

Why all the secrecy? Isn't foraging about sharing free food and swapping information and ideas with like-minded people? Well yes, but there's a limit, and revealing the whereabouts of my best London wild garlic patch definitely goes beyond it. Not only is this secluded woodland location free from dogs (and what they leave behind them) but I know that the soil quality here is excellent and has been relatively recently tested. This information allows me to not only gather and consume as much of this wonderful plant as I like, but also dig up its bulbs without worrying they may have absorbed anything unpleasant from the ground. As a general rule, I move around a lot, eating the city plants that I forage from as wide a spread of locations as possible. Rules, however, were made to be broken and the abundance of wild garlic that I found growing there today, coupled with a healthy dose of greed, left me no choice but to gather a huge bag of leaves, stems and even a few tiny green and white flowers. In a few weeks' time I could return to collect the seed heads, just as the petals were dropping off, and use them to make wild garlic capers. The bulbs could be dug and pickled later in the year but for now my attentions were focused on the strong-smelling bright green foliage I'd collected, most of which I would sweat for a couple of minutes and freeze to use throughout the year. I'd already decided to make a batch of wild garlic pakoras but, as so often happens, I bumped into another plant and it invited itself round for dinner. Although there are a couple of vague similarities, ground ivy is in the Mint family and not remotely related to the poisonous creeper that grows all over cemeteries and woodlands. Complex would be the only way to describe the smells and tastes of this low-growing, rambling little plant, a mix of lavender, mint, sage, thyme and rosemary, with a good waft of hemp thrown in. It's not to everyone's taste but I adore it and often make a tea from it, either on its own or blended with varieties of wild mint. I've also used it to make fritters, pakoras, muffins and pancakes, all of which benefit from its similarities to sage.

Ground ivy and wild garlic pakoras

100g ground ivy leaves (and stems if tender enough), 50g wild garlic leaves and stems, 2 green chillies, 1 onion, 250g potatoes, 2 tsp salt, 1 tsp ground turmeric, 1 tsp garam masala, 350g chickpea flour (also called gram flour), a good frying oil, preferably coconut

Most things will taste great when you add salt and chilli, then batter and deep-fry them, but the aim with all my cooking is to allow natural flavours to do most of the work and use the other ingredients to enhance, rather than smother them. Fortunately, with ground ivy and wild garlic, we have two very strong-tasting greens that will hold their own regardless of which spices they are cooked with. This recipe makes about twenty pakoras; it sounds like a lot but they will go very quickly.

Roughly chop the ground ivy leaves (and stems if tender) and the wild garlic leaves and stems. Finely chop and deseed the green chillies and finely chop the onion. Mix all these ingredients together and then dice and parboil the potatoes. Add these to the mix along with the salt, turmeric powder and garam masala.

In a separate bowl, mix the chickpea flour with just enough water so that the batter will hold its consistency when dripped off the back of a spoon. Now mix the contents of both bowls together and, if you have the patience, leave to stand for an hour or so, before heating a good-sized pan with about 10cm of oil. Test the oil is hot enough by dropping in a spot of the batter – it should sizzle immediately – and then cook the pakoras by frying heaped tablespoons of the mixture, giving them about 5 minutes in the oil until they turn a golden brown. Leave on a paper towel to drain off any excess oil before serving, ideally with a crunchy wild flower salad and a dip made by mixing plain yogurt and mint sauce.

MINER'S LETTUCE
(WINTER PURSLANE)

Claytonia perfoliata

Five-petalled white flowers
growing from the centre of
the leaf, occasionally with
much smaller leaves just
beneath the flowers

Lower leaves on tips of long
stalks. When in flower the
leaf wraps around the stalk,
which joins in the centre

PARTS USED: Leaves (including stems), flowers

HARVESTING TIP: Take care as the leaves
bruise very easily

7th March. Southwark Park

So vast and densely populated is London that it's easy to miss things that are right under our noses. Sometimes you even discover a place that you have never visited before, despite its proximity to home. I spent today hunting for a location reasonably close to the Tate Modern gallery, somewhere suitable to take some of its staff on a wild food walk the following week. By midday I found myself, for the first time ever, in Southwark Park, sitting outside the cafe and drinking tea in glorious sunshine. An online search earlier had revealed a few interesting areas to look at, including a small lake and a nature reserve, both ideal spots for edible plants, but alas the water's edge was pretty bare and a bit muddy, ideal for ducks but not for me. The nature reserve looked more promising but it was bordered by imposing Victorian metal railings leading to a gate that was locked. Again, great for the wildlife but not so good for the urban forager. On the other side of the park a small area of unmanaged grassland revealed a few interesting plants, the usual seasonal suspects: yarrow, common mallow, dandelion, bittercress, hedge mustard and wild chervil. I also spotted a patch of familiar-shaped leaves, those of young evening primrose, growing in rosettes, close to the ground, a distinctive green with a white stripe running down the centre of each. This is a plant with numerous edible parts, including tasty roots, but tempting as it was, a London park is not the place to start digging up anything, even if it does appear to be growing wild.

Thwarted for a third time, I decided to leave, returning to the cafe to grab a take-away coffee, which I drank while milling about and trying to decide if there was enough here to interest the lovely people of the art world. Part thinking, part daydreaming, I realized I was staring across the road at a vast patch of light green, made up of almost perfectly circular leaves, topped with tiny white flowers. Not quite in focus, I flicked through a mental catalogue of available wild plants and stopped abruptly on the page marked winter purslane. As long as they're not doing any harm, I'm generally not bothered whether plants are native or not, grown intentionally, totally wild or garden escapees. I can only assume that this almost endless sea of green had been planted at some point but had decided to rebel against any attempts to contain it; it was now probably 75 metres across. After filling my trusty cloth bag I scrounged a couple of carrier bags from the cafe and filled them, too, then looked back at the patch, which appeared utterly unchanged by my recent harvest. Now, what to do with a glut of this delicious crispy plant?

Winter purslane pesto and numerous other ideas

1 cup almonds, winter purslane, olive oil, bunch of sorrel leaves (optional), juice of 1 lemon, 1–2 tsp salt, about 3 tbsp grated parmesan

On the group forays I run, I sometimes find myself saying, 'Tasty as this is, I wouldn't want to eat a whole plateful of it.' Wild foods can have wild flavours and often need using in moderation – not so with winter purslane, also known as miner's lettuce (so called because it was consumed in great quantities to prevent scurvy during the American gold rush) and perhaps most romantically referred to as spring beauty. Packed with vitamin C, this is a plant with crunchy sweet-tasting leaves and stems, making it an ideal base for a salad and equally good as the sole ingredient.

To make a simple pesto, blitz the almonds in a blender until they are finely chopped, then fill it to the top with winter purslane leaves and stems and blend until the greenery becomes a paste, adding a splash of olive oil to help lubricate it. Then, if you have them, repeat this process with a big bunch of sorrel leaves and if you don't, add more winter purslane followed by the lemon juice and another good slug of olive oil. Now add the salt and a few heaped tablespoons of freshly grated parmesan, unless you are planning to freeze the mixture, in which case leave the cheese out and add it later.

Stored in sterilized jars, this will keep in the fridge for a few weeks. The basic recipe is easy to adapt for numerous other wild greens, working especially well with wild garlic or wild rocket. Used in soups, winter purslane can substitute or combine well with spinach, nettles and all other greens, wild or otherwise. It will also add depth to a hearty chicken soup and bring colour and flavour to home-made pasta or gnocchi. As a cooked green, it tastes like a gentle spinach, requires very little heat to wilt and seems to go with just about everything, but my most common approach to this plant, especially when faced with a decent quantity, is to shove it in the blender with some apple juice and use it as a base for a wild green smoothie (see January's recipe on page 16 for more details on this).

HOGWEED

Heracleum sphondylium

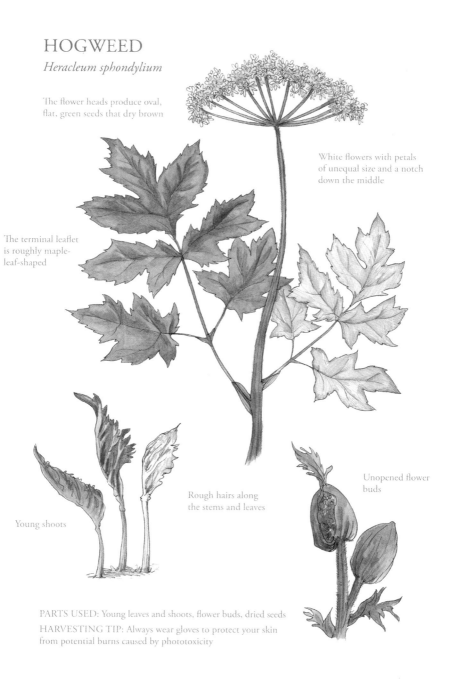

The flower heads produce oval, flat, green seeds that dry brown

White flowers with petals of unequal size and a notch down the middle

The terminal leaflet is roughly maple-leaf-shaped

Unopened flower buds

Young shoots

Rough hairs along the stems and leaves

PARTS USED: Young leaves and shoots, flower buds, dried seeds

HARVESTING TIP: Always wear gloves to protect your skin from potential burns caused by phototoxicity

15th March. Primrose Hill

Not only is the city I live in blessed with a multitude of open and green spaces, some of them have stunning views. On a clear day standing at the top of Alexandra Palace Park it's possible to see the transmitter at Crystal Palace fifteen miles to the south, with the whole city laid out in between. Today I had an early meeting with a baker in Camden Town, keen to discuss the idea of incorporating some foraged flavours into some of their speciality breads. We arranged to take a walk together the following month, when there would be more to show her. Leaving her to get on with her day, I walked towards Primrose Hill, crossing the top end (the wild bit) of Regent's Park, partly to see what I could forage for en route and partly to take in the view on this early spring day. In the distance lay the now classic London skyline, punctuated by landmark buildings – the Shard, the Gherkin, the London Eye and lastly the BT Tower, a building that changes its name every few years but always looks exactly the same. Between the skyscrapers (do people still call them that?) and my vantage point were some of London's most famous districts – Mayfair, Soho and Marylebone – and in front of them I could see Regent's Park and the top of the Snowdon Aviary at London Zoo. But all this sight-seeing wasn't getting me anything to eat so I pulled my focus back to the land right in front of me.

Crossing the manicured grass at the top of the hill, it gave way to what would soon become a huge wild flower meadow, although for now, this early in the year, it was mostly a mix of young winter greenery and stinging nettles. On closer examination I was delighted (yes, delighted) to find the young 'fiddle head'-shaped growth of one of my favourite plants, common hogweed. These unfurled shoots were all between 2 and 4 inches high, the perfect time to pick them, and currently presenting only one danger to the unprepared forager, nestled as they were among thousands of very young stinging nettles. I don't really mind getting stung, it comes with the territory, and getting a bit carried away while picking is one of the true joys of foraging.

I managed roughly one sting for every dozen shoots, so after gathering about half a kilo my hands were throbbing, and I headed home to cook and apply some handcream.

Steamed and fried hogweed shoots

Hogweed, butter, salt and pepper

I admit it, 'steamed' or 'fried' are hardly the most innovative of recipe suggestions but these are my preferred ways to enjoy the young stems of this wonderful wild vegetable. Give me hogweed shoots fried in butter with salt and pepper or just steamed and dressed with a splash of soy sauce and I am a happy man. Tempura them and I am in wild food heaven. These shoots pop up any time from February onwards, depending on the weather, and, as with many members of the Carrot family, they have another flush towards the end of the year when they put up a second batch of shoots and leaves. Careful identification of all members of this group of plants is vital, poisonous lookalikes including hemlock lurk among the edible delights of fennel, wild carrot, wild chervil and sweet cicely. Fortunately hogweed is easy to identify, with bristly, much broader foliage than any of the poisonous varieties, although care is needed if collecting on a hot day; the sap can cause contact dermatitis in some people (resulting in painful blisters), as can any form of contact with its much larger relative, giant hogweed. As a rule of thumb, learn your carrots with someone who knows their stuff, not with a guidebook, and you will be on safe ground. And if it's a sunny day, always wear gloves to collect your hogweed shoots.

The young leaves of hogweed are great just dry-fried, they become crispy and taste like seaweed, and it's often possible to find plants with new growth on them throughout the spring and summer.

The next crop becomes available when the plants are forming their flowers, with the unopened flower heads growing close to the stem, wrapped in ribbed pods with a pinky purple tinge to them. Think of them as tiny cauliflowers or broccoli heads and cook them accordingly. I eat them just steamed for a couple of minutes but my friend Jason makes a mean hogweed cheese bake. Timing, as with all things in foraging, is important; too soon and they are too small, too late and they are flowering and the texture has become too fluffy.

The last crop to be harvested from hogweed is its seeds and, again, careful identification is needed due to their similarities with other members of this plant family, all of which produce umbrella-shaped flowers called umbels. These seeds, unlike its poisonous relatives, grow as almost perfectly formed little discs and once you have been shown them they are very easy to spot. Their flavour is intense; a strong orange taste mixes with bitterness and more complex back tastes, making them ideal in cocktails, for flavouring desserts or as an ingredient in biscuits and cakes.

BURDOCK

Arctium lappa

Produces a long taproot,
with tiny rootlets
coming off the sides.
Light brown on the
outside, white inside

Burs made of many hooked hairs
that stick to skin and clothing

The leaves are 10–50cm long –
wide at the base and with a
woolly underside

PARTS USED: Roots, flowering stems

HARVESTING TIP: Harvest the roots in the spring or autumn by digging a trench around
the plant then cutting out the centre and the roots with it

21st March. Mum's allotment garden in Hertfordshire

I am a terrible gardener; although my intentions are always good, I seem to lack the ability to follow through. When I had my own little allotment, actually just one raised vegetable bed in the grounds of my local climbing centre, even this proved too much work. The problem I have is not with what I'm growing, it's with all the other delicious plants that are constantly popping up elsewhere without any effort on my part. Foragers like to move around so being married to one spot just doesn't cut it and even when I had a house in rural Dorset, I abandoned my vegetable patch, finding that it filled up with wild and delicious burdock, requiring utterly no effort on my part other than digging them up. Today, as Mum was proudly showing me her new raised beds and the rows of vegetables they were producing, my attention began to wander a little. I was genuinely happy for her but as she pointed to carrots, onions, kale and potatoes, I found myself scanning a rather overgrown area about 30 feet away and, specifically, the dead stems of a huge patch of burdock. Many of us know this plant from the childhood drink, but the famous dandelion and burdock actually started life in the Middle Ages, and across the centuries morphed from an alcoholic root beer, similar to a mead, into the sweet kids' drink that is still available, although I doubt very much whether the contents of the present-day version have been anywhere near the roots of either plant. A robust thistle, burdock lives for just two years, and although the upper parts are extraordinarily bitter it produces an amazingly tasty root that is at its best in the autumn of its first year or the spring of its second.

After enthusing about Mum's productivity, I borrowed a spade and headed over to investigate, finding plenty of healthy new plants growing amongst the dead stems and burs of the previous year, their leaves thick and dark green, growing low to the ground and looking quite similar to those of rhubarb. The trick when digging up a burdock root is to dig a trench all around it, a doughnut shape in the soil, and then cut the middle and the root from the centre of it. Avoid the mid-winter and the summer: the ground is too hard and roots are best dug when the plants are putting their efforts into making healthy rootstock, not masses of foliage or flowers. Half an hour's digging and I had a couple of dozen roots resembling parsnips of varying sizes, some like small carrots and a few as big as my forearm. I have to wonder, why does nobody in the UK grow this wonderful root vegetable?

Burdock root 'four ways'

Burdock is a plant in two halves; the top is a powerful medicine, very bitter and excellent at helping to detoxify the liver. The bottom, although also very useful medically, is a truly unique and tasty vegetable. What does it taste like? It tastes like burdock, of course. Our tendency is always to compare one thing to another, to find a reference point to describe something unusual by comparing it to something less interesting, but with burdock this just won't work, it is its own thing. Want to know how it tastes? Go and dig some up, preferably with the permission of the person whose land it's growing on.

For the marinade: burdock root, 60ml rice wine vinegar, 60ml vegetable stock, 2 tbsp runny honey, 2 tbsp good-quality soy sauce, salt

For the stock: burdock root, butter or oil, onion, garlic, carrot, mixed herbs, soy sauce (optional), salt and pepper

There are numerous ways to cook burdock root, most simply to boil or roast it like you would any other root veg. Cutting it into thin fingers and boiling with water and a splash of soy sauce produces a vegetable dish that I think of as Chinese in flavour and Japanese in texture, or thin slicing and parboiling makes it ideal as a stir-fry ingredient.

To make marinated burdock root, a popular dish in Japan, clean and slice enough root to produce a couple of dozen finger-sized strips, then soak them in cold water for 5 minutes before parboiling them for another 5 minutes, making sure they are still crunchy. Now mix the rice wine vinegar with the stock, honey, soy sauce and a pinch of salt, bringing it all to the boil and adding the chopped roots for just a few seconds before taking it off the heat. Leave to marinate for 24 hours and if not quite tender enough, remove the roots and bash them with a rolling pin before returning them to the marinade for another 24 hours.

There are many other uses for burdock but why not try making a simple stock? Sauté the chopped roots in butter or oil, add salt and pepper, some chopped onion, garlic and carrot, a few mixed herbs (preferably wild ones) then add water and cook gently with the lid on for an hour or so. I'd probably also add some soy at the end but I tend to add soy sauce to almost everything.

SEA BEET

Beta vulgaris subsp. *maritima*

Clusters of tiny flowers on the long stem, with tiny leaves in between

Glossy leaves with wavy edges. Variable in shape and joining the stem alternately

Young leaves grow in sprawling clusters

PARTS USED: Leaves

HARVESTING TIP: Pluck the leaves and stems at the point at which they easily break, leaving any woody parts of the plant behind

27th March. Hanging from a cliff in Dorset

To be specific, I only spent the first half of the day precariously clinging to a cliff by my fingertips, and although I have occasionally climbed slightly 'off route' to examine the odd wild mushroom that was growing out of a rock face, I generally keep my climbing and foraging separate. Although my twin obsessions may not seem to have that much in common, there is definitely a meditative element to both. The act of hunting for food is ingrained on the human psyche and I often find myself 'zoning out' when quietly harvesting a patch of tasty wild plants. Non-climbers will be surprised to find out that a similar inner calm is achievable halfway up a sea cliff; like a series of complicated yoga poses, it's the mind that's really doing the work, not the body. Today was a perfect climbing day, sunny but not too hot, the rock dry and the air slightly crisp. We'd got out early and by mid-afternoon the four of us were driving along the coast, hungry from our exertions and already discussing ideas for dinner. A glimpse of dark green flickered in my peripheral vision and I shouted, a bit too dramatically, 'Stop the car!'

We pulled over next to a huge stretch of shingle beach and I explained to my companions that this was my favourite place to pick sea beet, an impressive and delicious wild spinach. Although this amazing coastal plant is very common, a direct ancestor of beetroot that grows in small tufts or big patches in most seaside areas, I have never seen anything like the 400–500-metre-long carpet of green that covers this stretch of shingle. Two winters ago, this whole coastline was decimated by storms and a large part of the beach was lifted into the air and thrown across the road, taking with it the sea beet and most of its root system. Just two years later and it's back with a vengeance, positively thriving and possibly bigger than ever. Nature is amazingly resilient, the only thing this plant can't cope with is people walking all over it and there was little to no chance of that in this neglected spot. I showed my friends how to collect it, giving each plant a haircut, taking the upper leaves and stems and leaving the base intact and able to produce new growth, which it will do pretty much all year round. Within minutes we had enough greenery to feed a small army of climbers and I threw down the gauntlet, declaring that for our dinner I was going to cook the world's tastiest-ever spinach dish.

Sea beet cooked with secret ingredients

Imagine a spinach that comes ready salted by nature, that doesn't reduce when cooked, that has thick leaves more similar to kale than the flimsy version they sell in the supermarket and that doesn't wilt on its own if left in the fridge for more than a day. Popeye was wasting his time with that tinned stuff; sea beet is what a real strongman should be eating! OK, that's enough wild food propaganda for now, let's get back to my boastful claims about creating the ultimate spinach dish.

Sea beet leaves, cheddar or feta cheese, soy sauce

This recipe was conceived to feed a group of hungry climbers a few years previously on holiday on Kalymnos, a Greek island that offers almost nothing by way of tourism except, you guessed it, climbing. On the only rainy day of this trip, we spent our time playing cards and eating our way through the menu of a local taverna, the whole group raving about how amazing the steamed spinach tasted. As happens with groups of competitive men (and women) we vowed to have some sort of contest to recreate it when we got home and there was much speculation about 'the secret ingredient'. The contest never happened but this would be my entry if ever it did.

First gather a bag of sea beet leaves, the ideal size for these should be about 10cm long but this will vary throughout the year. Give them a good wash and then steam them for about 6 minutes. Unlike domestic spinach, sea beet starts off a deep shiny green and part way through the cooking process it becomes almost black, turning a lovely green again when it's cooked. While it's steaming, it's time to prepare the secret ingredient: a good strong cheese. Mature cheddar or feta will both work well. Finely grate a few centimetres of your selected cheese then transfer the steaming hot sea beet to a bowl and quickly mix in enough of the cheese for it to completely melt and disappear. Remember, this is the secret bit, so leave no trace. Add as much cheese as possible without it becoming visible then add a good slug of soy sauce and mix this in too. The end result should look simply like steamed spinach but taste good enough to have everyone's eyes rolling and asking for more.

April

Magnolia petals lightly pickled in elderflower vinegar

White nettle 'risotto' with sumac and crispy garlic

Beech leaf and chilli infused vodka

Japanese knotweed and beech leaf punch

Cherry blossom syrup

'I walked the woods, running my hand along the length of just one low branch on every tree I passed, stripping the leaves and dropping them into my bag, almost silent, methodical, gently repetitive . . .'

MAGNOLIA
Magnolia x *soulangeana*

Furry buds produce
flowers 10–20cm
across, with six white
and pinkish-purple
petals

Large, smooth, oval leaves

PARTS USED: Flowers

HARVESTING TIP: Take care as the petals bruise easily

2nd April. Waterlow Park, Highgate

A dense and damp mist was hanging over most of the city this morning and Highgate, which looks like something of a time warp even without it, was positively Dickensian. For various random reasons I seem to have visited this park at regular intervals across the last twenty-five years, once for a picnic, once to break up with a girlfriend, once to clear my head after visiting a friend in the nearby hospital. Today, however, I was on 'official' business, meeting with the borough's ecology officer to discuss running a foraging event here. Her caution was understandable, this being a very beautiful and highly manicured little park. 'Why not just go to Hampstead Heath, it's full of wild plants, you know?' A valid question indeed, but it's the juxtaposition that really interests me, so I took her for a walk, around a place that she knows intimately, and slowly, gently, changed the way she would look at it forever. In roughly an hour, we looked at just over forty species of edible plants, wild and domestic, and we'd only covered a third of the park, getting nowhere near the designated wild area, a small but beautiful nature reserve. In just one spot I found spicy wild garlic, peppery cuckoo flower, sweet-scented lemon balm, wild carrot, winter cress, sweet cicely with a wonderful aroma of aniseed, wild spinach varieties, and so it went on. We looked, touched, rubbed, sniffed and tasted our way through the flower beds, borders and edges, before turning our attentions to the trees, too numerous to list. Her firm favourite, and biggest surprise, was discovering the complicated delights of eating magnolia petals. My work was done, the walk was approved and another person had been converted. I carefully collected a dozen of these amazing flowers, mindful that I was gathering the plant's reproductive organs and also careful to pick selectively so as not to spoil the view.

Magnolia petals lightly pickled in elderflower vinegar

Spring in a jar. These petals remind me of ginger and also of celery with a bitter hint of chicory, a delicate and complicated flavour indeed. A wild salad has as many surprises as it has ingredients, so some thin slices of magnolia are a great addition. There are over 200 varieties; mostly in the UK they are deciduous trees and a few evergreens, but I find the taste and texture very similar in all the species I have so far tried. I recently used dried and powdered magnolia petals as an excellent substitute spice when making my son some gingerbread biscuits. They were a terrific success, all consumed the same day. Magnolia can also be used as the base of a floral wine or a fragrant sorbet, but I think there are many more, untapped possibilities for this wonderfully complex ingredient. I find it flowering abundantly in the city from as early as mid-February, so as well as including it in the creation of my wild chai recipe (page 154), I have it in mind to experiment with it as a seasoning for fish cakes, maybe even home-made burgers or sausages.

3 tbsp elderflower vinegar (or 2 tbsp white wine or cider vinegar),
2 tbsp sugar, magnolia blossoms

For this super recipe I used last year's sweet-scented elderflower vinegar, made simply by leaving half a dozen elderflower sprays in vinegar for a week or so until it takes up their wonderful fragrance. You could just use a white wine or cider vinegar but it will need diluting quite a bit to not overpower the blossoms.

Play with the quantities above but my version is to gently heat the elderflower vinegar or white wine vinegar and sugar together with about 6 tablespoons of water then leave to cool before adding to roughly enough petals to fill a standard-sized glass jar. They are ready to eat just 12 hours later and, surprisingly, these delicate flowers keep for ages – the colour gets lost but the taste does not. Alternatively, pickle them in rice vinegar and soy; a great recipe for this version is on Robin Harford's brilliant website www.eatweeds.co.uk. I add them to salads, serve them with cheese or cold meats, or just munch a few each time I walk past the jar.

WHITE DEAD NETTLE

Lamium album

White flowers with hairy upper
lip and notched lower lip

Square stems

Coarsely toothed leaves
with pointed tips
occurring in opposite
pairs, each at 90 degrees
to the next

PARTS USED: Leaves, flowers
HARVESTING TIP: Pick only the tips for salads. Think 'mushroom' when tasting the flowers

15th April. Burgess Park

Our Royal Parks are the beautifully manicured jewels in London's green crown, and a must-see for any visitor to the city. So which one would I take a visitor to – Regent's Park, Greenwich Park, Hyde Park, Green Park? To be honest, probably none of the above: London has so many less-grandiose patches of green, focal points for local communities, more for everyday use than the 'best china' feeling I get from the big four. Imagine a city park that is all things to all people – wide open spaces for sports, tennis courts, a decent cafe with sensible prices, a venue for hire, community food, growing projects, allotments and gardens, a well-thought-out and safe playground, an undulating landscape instead of just flat grassland. Add to this a big lake where fishing is allowed, some woodland, huge flower meadows and wild areas, a running track and even a couple of dozen built-in barbecues . . . welcome to Burgess Park. It has relatively recently been revamped with funds from the national lottery and it's one of my favourite places in the whole city. Were I to live closer, I would spend all my time there but today, like so many of my visits, was a brief one, just an hour to spare, affording me enough time for a coffee and a wander through the meadows, currently exploding with colour and springtime exuberance. A wild flower meadow, albeit a managed one, creates such a marvellous contrast to its urban setting, calming to the brain, easy on the eye and slowing down the pace of city life from a sprint to a gentle stroll. I drifted around, surrounded by yellow and white ox-eye daisies, newly emerging deep green rocket leaves, white tufts of yarrow and the first of the deep red poppies, but time got the best of me, the phone rang, the spell was broken and I had to dash away.

Faced with so much beauty and such variety, without my usual collecting bag, I almost forgot to pick anything at all, but not wanting to leave empty handed, I grabbed a few dozen tempting-looking stems from a patch of one of my favourite city plants – white dead nettle. Unrelated to the stinging nettle, lacking its stinging hairs, and very much alive, this is a member of the Mint family with delicious leaves and flowers available all year round. I took roughly the top 6 inches, which were light green and tender with rings of white flowers growing close to the stem. If nothing else, I had the inspiration for tonight's dinner.

White nettle 'risotto' with sumac and crispy garlic

300–400g white nettle or stinging nettle tops, half a dozen spring onions, 2 garlic cloves, olive oil, 200g long-grain rice, sumac powder, fried garlic, fried seeds (optional), salt and pepper

Serves 2–3

Wild food can be classy food, too, as I remind everyone when the porcini mushroom season comes around. This recipe includes the lovely citrus-tasting buds of the stag horn sumac tree and although they won't come into flower until later in the year, they are not uncommon in the city. Obviously I'd encourage you to pick your own, but in the meantime, sumac powder is readily available in the shops or on the internet. If you'd like to use stinging nettles instead of the non-stinging white dead nettle, you'll need to get your rubber gloves on to pick and cook them.

Wash and roughly chop the nettle tops but remove the white dead nettle flowers first and keep them for the end. Drop them into about 600ml boiling water for a couple of minutes until they wilt, then drain but keep the water for later.

Finely chop the spring onions and garlic cloves (or any wild garlic varieties you might have) and fry gently in some olive oil, then add the long-grain rice. Stir it for a minute, then add the nettles and twice the volume of the reserved nettle water to rice, covering and simmering it for 10–12 minutes.

When the rice is cooked, season and sprinkle with sumac powder, crispy fried garlic and any other savoury seeds you fancy. Finally, add the flowers of the white dead nettle as a beautiful garnish. To me they taste just like little mushrooms – strange but true.

BEECH
Fagus sylvatica

Smooth leaves with
white hairs along their
edges and pointed tips

The hairy outer case splits
into four parts to reveal
two nuts

PARTS USED: Leaves, nuts

HARVESTING TIP: Strip just a single low stem of
young leaves from each tree and move on to the next

16th April. Near, but not in, Epping Forest

I can think of no greater foraging pleasure than the simplistic and singular task of gathering young beech leaves. A beech forest is a place of calm, part wild but with its own clear sense of order in the natural spacing of the trees, the symbiotic relationships between the woodlands and the fungi that help manage them, the subtle lift in temperature that the forest canopy creates and helps contain. Alas, we have only 2 per cent of our ancient woodland left in the UK so I always feel a huge sense of privilege at being able to walk through such a wonderful part of our landscape, and today was no exception, sunny, slightly chilly, perfect foraging weather. I say my purpose was singular but in all honesty, this is never the way for the enthusiastic forager, constantly aware of what is and what isn't available, looking for the expected, finding the unexpected, always searching. The newly emerged beech leaves are pale yellow, translucent and edged with soft, fluffy hairs, drooping downwards from their branches in opposite pairs, tens of thousands of them adorning each enormous tree. I walked the woods, running my hand along the length of just one low branch on every tree I passed, stripping the leaves and dropping them into my bag, almost silent, methodical, gently repetitive. On autopilot, my brain free to wander, I allowed my hands to fill my bag over a period of about an hour, gathering my bounty but leaving no trace of my visit, and no impact on my surroundings, visible or otherwise. At the same time, my eyes were working on the secondary purpose of my visit, to hunt for early St George's mushrooms or, failing that, signs that they might be on their way. This time I found neither, but was very happy with my haul of deliciously soft leaves, and with their delicate lemony tang they already had me thinking of the various ways I could put them to use.

Beech leaf and chilli infused vodka

Beech leaves, 1 bottle of vodka, 250g sugar, green and red medium-strength chillies

For many years I have made the classic forager's drink with these leaves, a beech noyau, using gin, sugar and brandy. The result is a deliciously sweet and warming digestif that becomes more flavoursome with age and is the perfect thing to nip from a hip flask on a chilly autumn mushroom hunt, possibly in the same woods the leaves were gathered from. When I opened the cupboard to hunt for some gin in which to infuse my most recently gathered beech leaves, and found only vodka, I decided it was time for a change.

This recipe is simplicity itself and starts with a large kilner jar or similar vessel. Fill this with young beech leaves, packing in as many as possible, then pour in a whole bottle of vodka, making sure the leaves are covered; add a little water or more vodka if needed. Now leave it to infuse for three weeks, giving it a stir or a prod every so often, turning over the top leaves if they are protruding above the surface. Then strain out the leaves and add sugar water, made by warming 300ml water and dissolving the sugar in it. Dependent on the size of the bottles you intend to decant into, there should be about two bottles' worth. I use clear glass with swing tops and into each I add one green and one red medium-strength chilli, deseeded and cut lengthwise into strips. Within 24 hours they have done their work but my last batch is over two years old and they are still in there, admittedly looking rather sad.

The flavour of this drink 'comes at you' in three different waves; the sweetness and lemon first, then the medicinal and cleansing feel from the vodka and finally, on the back, a lovely warm chilli heat, which as the drink ages, changes to more of a capsicum taste . . . complex stuff, or so a friend who works as a wine-maker told me.

JAPANESE KNOTWEED

Reynoutria japonica

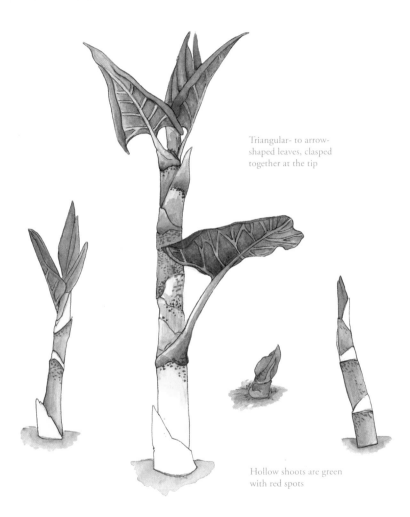

Triangular- to arrow-
shaped leaves, clasped
together at the tip

Hollow shoots are green
with red spots

PARTS USED: Young shoots

HARVESTING TIP: Select young, tender stems no higher than 30cm. It is illegal to spread
this plant, so be mindful of the law and common sense

19th April. A neighbour's back garden

As I've said, I know little to nothing about gardening and other than growing some green veg every so often, it's just not something I do. In fact, I gave up my small allotment plot because I was always busier picking the wild plants growing around it than the domestic ones in it. This utter lack of knowledge doesn't stop my neighbours using me as a plant ID service every time something unusual pops up in their gardens, and over the years I have learnt some of the language of the gardener, primarily so as to be able to communicate with a greater audience during the events I run. They say aconite, aquilegia and delphinium, while I would prefer to call these three wolfsbane, columbine and larkspur; when talking wild plants and their historical uses, it's always more interesting, more informative and just more romantic to use their traditional, sometimes bizarre, names. Who wants to call a plant polygonum when you can use the more descriptive title water pepper, or infinitely better than both, the old English name, Arsesmart! Today I found myself in a neighbour's back garden, with my three-year-old son Oscar, shouting loudly and running around excitedly, while I tried to work out how to break the news. My opening gambit: 'Well, the good news is that it's edible and very tasty.' I knew exactly what the thirty or so pinky purple spears emerging from the ground were, so reluctantly I told him that we were looking at the dreaded Japanese knotweed, an invasive plant of such destructive powers that it can grow straight up through the pavement, destabilize walls and sometimes render a property uninsurable. With no natural predators in the UK to keep it in check, this plant really is a menace, albeit a very tasty one. I suggested he contact the council, who have very strict rules governing its removal and irradiation, but only after I'd picked a bunch of shoots to take home with me.

Japanese knotweed and beech leaf punch

Imagine a very good rhubarb with the addition of a sharper, more lemony tang – not only is it very tasty but Japanese knotweed is a very versatile plant, too. I have enjoyed such delights as J. K. and apple crumble, J. K. jelly and J. K. flapjacks, and today's invention, Japanese knotweed and beech leaf punch, using a few tender knotweed shoots no longer than about 10 inches and some of the leftover beech leaves from my recent woodland walk.

6–12 Japanese knotwood shoots, 2 big handfuls of beech leaves, white sugar or pale honey, juice of 1 lemon

This punch is lovely on its own with ice, but also goes well with sparkling water or with chopped fruit or berries added. It could just as easily be made fizzy with a shot of CO_2 from a Soda Stream.

Chop the knotweed shoots and cook them together with the young lemony beech leaves in about 1.5 litres of water for 20 minutes. Then stir in some sugar or honey (to taste) and the lemon juice, cool the liquid, strain it and put it in the fridge for 24 hours.

The result, a truly delicious, and original, spring drink, but before deciding to gather Japanese knotweed I would seriously suggest you consider the damage caused by this massively invasive plant and be sure you harvest carefully and responsibly, having read some of the guidelines online. If in any doubt, this recipe works well with just beech leaves or you could use domestic rhubarb instead, but only a little so you don't overpower the delicate beech flavours. If you'd like to try making a crumble instead, skip forward to September's blackberry section (page 176) and adapt it accordingly – the addition of super-sweet crème de cassis in this recipe will work wonders with the fruity sharpness of the Japanese knotweed.

CHERRY
Prunus avium

Finely toothed oval leaves

The flowers have five white petals with many stamens visible, 2cm across

Smooth bark with many horizontal lines

PARTS USED: Flowers, fruit

HARVESTING TIP: Most wild cherries are a bit disappointing – leave them for the birds and concentrate on the blossoms

27th April. Kensal Green

Although an urban family, we spend more time outdoors than most people; the mix of foraging, children's activities and my wife Ellie's work as a photographer gives us numerous reasons to leave the house and the omnipresent seduction of computer screens. Today we visited friends across town, at just six or seven miles away; a journey of this sort can take on epic proportions in the city, but today was a Sunday, we were out early and all the traffic hadn't got out of bed yet. Our friends have two young sons so we headed to their local park, the kids going feral, allowing the adults to relax, drink coffee and catch up. Although the park is a place where most people can turn off some of their senses and dial down the machinations of their busy brains, for me it is not, it's just too full of fascination. A gorgeous avenue of mature cherry trees was calling to me, resplendently swamped with bright pink blossoms, running from almost one side of the park to the other. So grabbing what came to hand, two plastic buckets intended for playing in the sand pit, I went for a wander and gathered as many petals as I could fit into each one, munching a few as I walked. Cherry blossom can taste of three things – sweet, bitter or a delicious almond oil essence – and will often deliver a combination of these in no apparent order. The expression 'suck it and see' is very apt. Later I was forced to give up the buckets and decant my blossoms into the hood of Ellie's coat for the journey home.

Cherry blossom syrup

Of the many varieties of wild cherry I come across, most are a bit sour or have more stone than fruit. Even if you're lucky enough to find a sweet variety, the birds often strip the trees before they ripen. Cherry blossom, on the other hand, is a far more reliable and plentiful crop, and in Japan it's harvested commercially to make a

similar syrup to this recipe. One of the earlier spring blossoms, it appears from early March until early May with all of the UK varieties being suitable, even the ornamental ones. Making syrup means you don't need to be too careful, it doesn't matter if the blossom breaks up, and the variety doesn't matter either, but if picking in any quantity, avoid taking from just one tree.

Cherry blossom, brown or white sugar

A carrier bag half full of loosely packed blossom is plenty for a batch of syrup. First remove as many leaves and bits of debris as possible, then bring a pan of water to the boil, just enough to cover all the petals, but don't add them yet. Let the water cool to about 80°C or you'll 'burn' the flowers, ending up with an unpleasant taste. Now pour the hot water over the blossom, just enough to cover, and leave for 24 hours before straining using a jelly bag or fine sieve. Squeeze the blossom to get maximum flavour, then discard and bring the infused water to a boil, reducing the liquid a little to increase the flavour.

Measure the liquid and dissolve the sugar in it at a 1:1 ratio, i.e. into 500ml of liquid dissolve 500g sugar. You may want to experiment with less sugar or adding honey or xylitol instead, but either way you will be rewarded with a wonderful almondy syrup that's as delicious on vanilla ice cream as it is served as a sauce with red meat.

(Recipe courtesy of fellow forager Peter Studzinski.)

May

Deep-fried leaf crisps with chilli and salt

A salad with lime leaves, yarrow, fennel
and ox-eye daisy

Nettle beer

Water mint ice cream

Watercress soup

*'Many years from now I will remember this day, based entirely
on its smell, the strong and sweet odour of mint, with a waft of
turpentine thrown in – this is the smell of water mint . . .'*

BEECH
Fagus sylvatica

HAWTHORN
Crataegus monogyna

SILVER BIRCH
Betula pendula

ENGLISH OAK
Quercus robur

HARVESTING TIP: Select very young leaves,
pale yellow to light green and often slightly translucent

3rd May. Springfield Park

It was hot, really deliciously hot, that weekend in early May where the weather pretends it's mid-summer for a few days before settling back to the seasonal norm of 'slightly disappointing'.

There are probably 250 wild and not so wild plants in my urban repertoire, it may be more, I've never properly counted. Add to that at least the same amount from the hedgerows and the coast, plus numerous edible seaweeds and mushrooms. The list is enormous and the culinary possibilities are endless, so why should I find myself, at such a fertile point in the year and, unusually for me, with time on my hands, struggling to think of what turn my wild food journey should take next? I really have no idea. Perhaps the luxury of having time to think and the sheer abundance of what was available was all a bit too much, when most of my decisions, recipes and ideas are made, very much, 'on the hoof'. As I often do, I was picking a wild salad, wandering and selecting only the most tempting-looking greens, mulling over ideas but finding no real inspiration, until I randomly wondered if I could batter and deep-fry everything I had collected and how it would turn out. Pretty horrid, was the conclusion I reached, but now my brain was ticking and a nearby oak tree was calling to me. Eureka! Leaf crisps! Why had I never made these before?

Deep-fried leaf crisps with chilli and salt

Young birch, beech and oak leaves, oil, salt, chilli powder

I say 'deep', but the method I adopted was a halfway house between deep- and shallow-frying, using a small saucepan and a few centimetres of oil, the same way I have always cooked seaweed. Having dry-fried numerous wild greens in the past, usually to make savoury sprinkles to add to my food, it's bizarre that this penny had never dropped before.

I'd collected a few varieties of tree leaves that I knew to be edible, or at least to not be toxic (so no trying this with the needles of the poisonous yew tree), including birch, beech, oak, hawthorn and linden, and experimented with each, getting varying results. The hawthorn were too tough and a little bitter, but this is a tasty leaf earlier in the year so I put this down to my poor timing, one to come back to. The linden was a disaster, as I expected, due to the high levels of mucilage, the substance that gives okra its signature sliminess – to say the least, they did not turn out well. The top three were the birch and beech, both of which have tender and opaque leaves at this time of year, and most surprisingly the oak. Oak trees contain high levels of tannin, also found to a lesser degree in red wine and black tea, a preservative with a bitter taste, normally far too drying for the human palate. Acorns require soaking in numerous changes of water before enough of their tannins have dispersed to make them usable as a food, after which they produce an excellent and versatile flour, a truly under-utilized wild resource. My oak leaves were very young, pale green and, as such, much less bitter than they would become later in the year. Even uncooked they tasted OK, but once they had spent 10–20 seconds in the pan, then were drained on kitchen paper and sprinkled with salt and a hint of chilli powder, they were simply delicious and looked stunning with their classic wavy edge.

OX-EYE DAISY
Leucanthemum vulgare

Large daisy-like flowers
with a firm yellow
centre and an outer ray
of white petals

Long-stalked lower leaves with rounded
teeth. Their shape changes significantly
higher up the flowering stem

Has a distinctive sweet
smell when broken

PARTS USED: Leaves, flowers

HARVESTING TIP: When picking the
young leaves be sure to avoid toxic Ragwort.
If in doubt wait until the plant flowers. Ragwort
will then be easy to identify with its yellow outer
petals as well as its yellow centre

8th May. Looking for new locations in the south of the city

Organizing urban foraging events is an excellent excuse to spend time in the capital's parks and green spaces, and under the vague guise of work I have visited more of them than anyone I know. Being slightly north-of-the-city-centric, I am often asked to run more walks 'south of the river', the city's physical and imaginary divide which seems to prevent even the most rational or socially mobile from crossing it. But today I made the transition without incident and spent the afternoon exploring the hidden wonders of Peckham, an astonishing little borough, counting twenty-three public green spaces in under two miles between Peckham Rye station and Burgess Park to the north. Like London in microcosm, it's just so much greener than we imagine it to be. En route, I collected random ingredients, the way you might from a big food shop, but without any specific recipe in mind, only realizing later that I had subconsciously assembled a delicious simple salad and a wonderfully calmative tea to drink after.

Lime leaf and ox-eye daisy has to be my favourite spring salad and usually I keep it to just these two ingredients with a splash of rose hip vinegar. Today, however, I also had fennel and yarrow in my bag; with their feathery foliage, both were at their absolute best in terms of sweetness of flavour and softness of texture. Fennel is perhaps the most scarce of these four in the city, but the ox-eye daisy is very common, and although in urban areas I tend to find its cultivated versions, they're usually as tasty as its wild relatives, with delicious fruity leaves and yummy-scented flowers. Look out for great big daisies about 2 to 3 feet high with yellow and white flowers (but don't eat any with entirely yellow flowers, they will be poisonous lookalike ragwort).

The lime leaves I collected are the heart-shaped foliage of the common lime or linden tree, found in abundance in every London park, with numerous medicinal properties attributed to both the leaves and flowers. The blossoms are used to make calmative tea, a treatment for stress and mild anxiety, while the leaves contain mucilage, a slimy substance that amongst other things helps suppress the cough reflex, so makes its way into home-made and commercially produced cough mixtures. I picked young, slightly translucent new-growth leaves, munching a few of the bigger ones, too, selecting them from a height that even the most enthusiastic dog could not manage to wee on. The blossoms, not out yet, have the wonderful taste of honeydew melon; dried, they make one of the best-tasting of all the herbal teas.

A salad with lime leaves, yarrow, fennel and ox-eye daisy

Let's be honest, generally when a book describes a plant's best use as 'making a great tea', it means it's rather dull and has no other merit. Not so for yarrow and fennel, two amazing-tasting herbs, packed with flavour and numerous medicinal and culinary attributes. Yarrow stimulates the appetite and aids digestion and I like to chew it when I have a sore throat. As a novice herbalist I use it for any and all ailments and in the kitchen as a salad, a cooked green veg and as a dried herb slightly similar to sage.

Fennel is one of nature's best calmatives as well as containing anethole, a powerful aromatic compound also found in camphor and anise, antimicrobial and anti-fungal. Both plants are diuretic, so help to cleanse and purify the body, which is ideal for us city-dwellers. Combined, they make my favourite of all the herbal teas and are both easy to ID: mature fennel with its tall bluish stems, yellow umbrella flowers and distinctive sweet smell and yarrow with its low clumps of feathery leaves. Even so, one is a member of the Carrot family and the other looks like it should be; as such I would recommend you initially get to know these two plants with someone knowledgeable rather than just using an ID book.

Lime leaves (and blossom), yarrow leaves, fennel leaves, ox-eye daisy, sweet vinegar or olive oil, lemon juice and salt (optional)

Rinse, dry and combine the leaves of all four plants, the flowers of the ox-eye daisy, and the lime blossoms, too, if you have them. Add a small splash of sweet vinegar but don't overpower these already wonderful flavours . . . Failing that, just use some olive oil and either a small splash of lemon juice or some salt, or both.

While we're on the subject of fennel, it's worth looking at a few of the other culinary uses of this wonderfully aromatic wild food. Any and all fish dishes can benefit from the herby sweetness this plant has to offer – fish cakes become elevated to a new level, baked trout takes on a more complex dimension and salmon cured with fennel stems, citrus fruits, coriander and black pepper knocks spots off your plain old smoked salmon. American foraging guru Green Deane recommends making a hearty pasta with penne, rigatoni, spicy Italian sausages and fennel stems while, closer to home, Devon's foremost authority on wild food, Robin Harford, suggests making a sweet seaside pickle using chopped fennel sprigs and marsh samphire. The possibilities are basically endless . . .

FENNEL
Foeniculum vulgare

An umbrella-shaped
flower head that divides
into smaller individual
flowers that are bright
yellow and each comprised
of five petals that curl in
on themselves

Deeply divided
leaves with soft,
thread-like leaflets

The seeds start off green,
tipped with yellow. They
turn to brown as they
mature and dry

Young foliage,
soft and bushy

PARTS USED: Leaves, flowers, seeds

HARVESTING TIP: Be 100 per cent
sure of your ID with young plants. Let
that delicious aniseed smell be your guide

15th May. Clissold Park, Stoke Newington

On this sunny May afternoon, armed with a big cloth bag, kitchen scissors and a pair of bright yellow rubber gloves, I headed for my favourite nettle bed (yes, I actually have a favourite patch of stingers), an almost endless sea of these delicious wild greens. At this time of year there's plenty of new growth coming through which I can use for making everything from nettle tempura (page 111), to a bright green protein-rich soup (page 104) or a spicy nettle aloo (page 137). But right now, it's time for nettle beer. This always sounded to me like a nasty concoction my dad might have forced upon us in the 1970s, a horrific hippy brew, low on taste and high on gas. How wrong I was: ready to consume in just over a week from picking, this amazing drink tastes like a cross between a wonderful rustic cider and an old-style ale or sweet wine.

To pick nettle tops, that's the upper 6–8 inches at this time of year, I usually use what I call the asparagus method, snapping the stem at the point at which it yields easily, moving up to the next leaf node and trying again if it doesn't, avoiding anything that looks damaged or dull, just collecting vibrant, healthy-looking leaves. For nettle beer I'm a bit less choosy and find it quicker and easier to just cut them off. So absorbing was the simplistic pastime of nettle collecting that I forgot quite how bizarre I must have looked as I stepped out of the undergrowth and back onto the path, frightening a group of joggers. Carrying a huge cloth bag slung around my neck and my bright yellow rubber hands brandishing a large pair of scissors . . . I was probably grinning, too! I apologized, explained myself and left the park quickly before the armed response unit turned up, or even worse the local residents association.

Nettles are a great 'cut and come again' plant, so if your local patch gets too tall, making the nettle tips too robust (and full of gritty crystals), you can cut them down and come back for the delicious new growth a few weeks later.

STINGING NETTLE

Urtica dioca

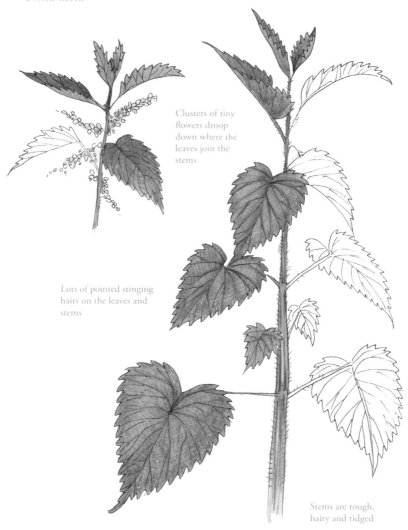

Clusters of tiny
flowers droop
down where the
leaves join the
stems

Lots of pointed stinging
hairs on the leaves and
stems

Stems are rough,
hairy and ridged

PARTS USED: Leaves, young stems, seeds

HARVESTING TIPS: Pick only the top 10–15cm of healthy, happy-looking
plants. Avoid the leaves when flowering. Wear gloves when needed

Nettle beer

This is the perfect drink for students, or anyone who's on a budget. As beers go it's very gentle but I'm never sure exactly how alcoholic it is (roughly 3 per cent ABV, I reckon); I have a hydrometer for measuring such things but rarely bother with anything so specific in any of my recipes.

Nettle tops, 500g white or brown sugar, 25g cream of tartar, 8g brewer's yeast

Take about fifty nettle tops (roughly the top 15–20cm of each should fill a carrier bag), picked as described above, wash them, still with your rubber gloves on, before adding to 6 litres of water (usually in two pans unless you have one huge one). Bring to the boil and simmer for 15–20 minutes before removing the nettles (eat them as a cooked veg or use to make a year's supply of nettle pesto) and adding the sugar and cream of tartar powder. Stir until the sugar dissolves and let the liquid cool to tepid before mixing in the brewer's yeast. Then leave, in a sterilized bucket with muslin over the top, for a few days before siphoning into sterilized bottles. If you have not done any siphoning before, this is the fun bit and just requires a length of clean plastic tube (you'll find plenty of demos on the internet but you can ignore most of what they say, it's really very simple). I usually leave my beer for five days but I have read of people leaving it up to two weeks. You need to let the first fermentation stage do its thing or your bottles will explode in dramatic fashion.

If you do fancy experimenting then try adding lots of grated fresh ginger to make a more spicy drink. This recipe makes about a dozen normal-sized bottles. To work out how alcoholic it is you could try drinking it all in one go and then compare this experience to drinking twelve shop-bought beers. Take notes, though, this is serious scientific research!

WATER MINT
Mentha aquatica

Clusters of tiny pink-purple
flowers, forming a rounded
'head' with long, protruding
stamens that are easily visible

Toothed and downy
oval-shaped leaves

PARTS USED: Leaves, flowers, young stems

HARVESTING TIP: Remember to always cook plants picked at the water's
edge (see the safety notes section on page 261 for more information)

25th May. The River Test, Hampshire

As summer approaches, many of the spring salads begin to turn woody and a little too bitter, while the autumn fruits and fungi are still a long way off. Where then should we head for the best foraging opportunities? Ideally the most mixed environment possible, which makes an estuary an excellent place to visit; the land meets the sea meets the river and with them a huge variety of seaweeds and sea beets, salt-marsh plants like samphire and purslane, and river's-edge plants like meadowsweet and comfrey. Although I didn't quite make it to the coast today, I did manage to subvert a trip to visit the in-laws, turning it into a wild food walk, ambling along the riverbank, looking at the wildlife and picking a few delicious edible plants to cook up later. When I'm back in the city, I crave the pace that a riverside walk imposes on me, the proximity to the water and its gentle movement, time slowing down a little and the family getting the chance to be just that, to chat about nothing in particular and enjoy the balance that comes from having all age groups present. Some events are instantly frozen in time, memories even before they've finished happening; with a saturated colour palette of low sunlight, reflections kicking off rippling water and the gentle shush of a breeze as it teased the tops of the reeds, today's walk was exactly this. But most vivid of all, many years from now I will remember this day, based entirely on its smell, the strong and sweet odour of mint, with a waft of turpentine thrown in – this is the smell of water mint.

Water mint ice cream

On its own, this is a great herb to serve with freshwater fish, especially trout, which I like to bake in foil, stuffed with water mint and ground ivy (which prefers to grow on riverside paths rather than the actual banks). How do you know it's water mint? It grows by or in the water and it looks and smells like mint, actually quite similar to peppermint in both appearance and fragrance.

20 sprigs of mint, 5 tbsp caster sugar, 375g crème fraiche, 3 egg whites, green food colouring (optional)

I found this recipe in a lovely book by Adele Nozedar called *The Hedgerow Handbook*, packed with simple and tasty ideas and beautiful illustrations.

Wash the sprigs of mint thoroughly then blanch in boiling water for a few seconds. As with any water's-edge plant, this step is a vital safety measure and will kill any parasites present (more information in the watercress section on page 104 and the chapter on safety on page 261). Now whizz the mint in a blender with the caster sugar, transfer to a bowl and stir in the crème fraiche. In a separate, clean bowl, whisk the egg whites to 'soft peaks' (this bit takes bloody ages) and fold them carefully into the mixture. I also added a bit of green food colouring. Transfer the mixture to a plastic container and put this into the freezer, stirring every half hour or so with a fork, to avoid it crystallizing (unless you're lucky enough to own an ice-cream maker which can do this for you). Obviously this recipe works with other types of mint, too.

WATERCRESS
Nasturtium officinale

Four-petalled white flowers with clusters of unopened buds at the tips of the stems

Dark green leaves, made of 2–4 pairs of leaflets and a terminal leaflet. No teeth

White trailing roots on the hollow main stem

PARTS USED: Leaves, flowers, young stems

HARVESTING TIP: Drop some leaves with the rootlets attached into the water so they can root further downstream. Always cook plants picked from the water or water's edge (see the safety notes section on page 261 for more information)

26th May. Reluctantly returning to the city

Don't get me wrong, I love this city, but sitting in a traffic jam for three hours in order to get back to it is not my idea of fun. Fortunately, Ellie has the ability to be rational about these things; when all I see is a national conspiracy designed with the sole purpose of giving me back ache, she perceives an opportunity and a chance to explore a bit of the countryside that we usually only whizz straight past. I'm not entirely sure where we ended up, but I was delighted to be there, swapping the frustrations of stationary vehicles for the delights of rolling fields, flower meadows and another riverbank, our second in as many days. Time spent by the river always reminds me of being on holiday as a child, trying but failing to catch a trout and always ending up waist-deep in the water. Today I had no fishing rod with me and I saw no fish, but the water quality was good, as indicated by the land around it supporting a diverse range of wild flowers and, more importantly, huge floating pontoons of one of my favourite wild foods, watercress. This delicious member of the cabbage family is available in various stages of growth almost all year round – I have even harvested some when there was snow on the ground. Thankfully, today was hot and sunny, becoming a perfect late spring day the second we left the rest of humanity behind. We sat on the grass and ate a makeshift picnic, more motorway services than wild food buffet, but old habits die hard and ten minutes later, having successfully gathered a huge bag of watercress, I was up to my waist in the river, sodden but happy. We sat in the sun by the river while we waited for the traffic to die down and for my clothes to dry out.

Watercress soup

Watercress is a close relative of the nasturtium and thrives in slightly alkaline running water, preferring a clean environment, so often its presence is a sign of decent water quality. Having said that, it is vital to NEVER eat this or any other water-growing or water's-edge plants raw, unless you can 100 per cent trace the water source, to be certain it doesn't run through any agricultural land. How do you do this? I do not know so I ALWAYS cook plants like watercress. The reason for this is to avoid ingesting a nasty little parasite called liver fluke which comes from sheep and cattle dung, lives on wild water plants and can be harmful if it gets inside you alive. And now the good news: cooking it kills it and renders it harmless, but no nibbling the odd raw leaf as you forage; rely on your eyes and your sense of smell (a good cressy cabbage aroma is what you're after). And now that's out of the way, back to the recipe . . . watercress soup is easy, quick and tastes wonderful.

Butter, olive oil, 1 onion, 4 medium potatoes, 2 litres vegetable or chicken stock, 3 large bunches of watercress, crème fraiche or single cream, salt and pepper, croutons, grated cheddar

This is a traditional recipe that has been through many pairs of hands and had many tweaks and changes along the way.

Heat a good knob of butter and a splash of oil in a big pan, chop and gently fry the onion, then add the potatoes, either cubed or sliced. Cook on a low heat for a few minutes before adding three-quarters of the stock and simmering for 15 minutes. Chop and add the watercress and after another 10 minutes put it all in a blender (or don't, it's up to you). Add the remaining stock or leave it out, depending on what thickness of soup you prefer. Lastly add a few good spoons of crème fraiche or single cream and salt and pepper to taste. Serve either hot or cold with croutons and/ or grated cheddar floating on the surface.

June

An old-style lemonade with elderflower
and lemon balm

Stinging nettle tempura with a black mustard ponzu

Salt marsh pickles and salt marsh fish cakes

Seasonal 'wild' flower salad

Lime blossom champagne

'In about two minutes I counted eighteen different edible
plants and eight fruiting or edible flowering trees. Daisies,
nettles, mallow, three types of wild spinach, chickweed, rose
hips, plum, rowan, linden, blackthorn. A mirror image of
London, where every square inch is of value, here nature was
abundant, compact but still thriving . . .'

LEMON BALM
Melissa officinalis

White flowers with a
notched upper lip and
three-lobed lower lip

Leaves roughly egg- to oval-
shaped. Deeply toothed. Light
yellowish green in the sunlight

PARTS USED: Leaves, flowers
HARVESTING TIP: Pick on a
sunny day for the strongest aroma,
although that can be tricky with
English weather

5th June. Stoke Newington

Sunshine, blue skies, roadworks and traffic jams. I'm not a huge fan of summer in the city but I never tire of visiting my most local park, an old friend who keeps me sane and always has something interesting to say. Today he says just one word: blossom. Lime, elder, plum and hawthorn all combining to give soft, sweet wafts that come and go as I walk. It's the elder I'm most interested in today, with an idea already in mind; sometimes it's the act of foraging that gives birth to a new recipe, other days, like today, it's the recipe that leads me to hunt for what I need. With so many possible uses for elderflowers, I normally default to the simplest recipes I can think of and when something already tastes and smells so fragrant it would be a shame to smother it with too many other ingredients. This morning it was sunny, a perfect early June day, really, and the ideal time to pick these amazing blossoms, when they are at their sweetest and at their best. An elderflower cordial can succeed or fail entirely on what the weather is up to when the flowers are picked. I like the idea that anything made with these lovely summery blooms is a direct reflection of how the weather was that day. I'm always shocked by just how many elder trees we have in the capital; like so many other things, they hide in plain sight, until they erupt with creamy white blossoms. Identifying elderflower is simple and relies mostly on your nose; once you know that smell you don't forget it. As a footnote, rowan and dogwood both come out around the same time with vaguely similar, big white sprays of flowers but neither has the wonderful smell and both have very different leaves to elder. It's not that these two are particularly toxic, more that they will make a lousy cordial, or in my case, the oh so simple to make lemonade.

Heading home today, another plant grabbed my attention, an unassuming-looking patch of greenery begging to join the elderflowers in my bag. Lemon balm is a strongly perfumed relative of mint and, once smelt, its heady aroma is never forgotten. It was instantly obvious that I had found the missing ingredient for the drink I had in mind.

An old-style lemonade with lemon balm and elderflower

This old-style, flat lemonade is probably my favourite thing to make with elderflowers, but in the last few years I have also made elderflower champagne, elderflower Turkish delight, elderflower custard and elderflower fritters.

Alternative uses for lemon balm include roast chicken wrapped in sage and lemon balm leaves, lemon balm ice cream (simply adapt my water mint recipe on page 101), lemon balm infused vodka or simply as a replacement in any recipe requiring mint or basil.

8–12 elderflower sprays, 6–8 stems of lemon balm, 4–6 heaped tbsp sugar, 2 lemons

Simple is best! Take the elderflower sprays and the leaves of the lemon balm and put them into a large bowl or jug with 1–1.5 litres of water. Add the sugar or honey or any other syrup you fancy so long as it has a mild taste, then halve and squeeze the juice of one of the lemons and add it to the liquid. Throw in the squeezed lemon and put it all in the fridge for 24 hours, strain and taste. Depending on how aromatic your lemon balm leaves are, you may want to add the juice of the other lemon. This drink tastes and smells amazing, but remember to pick your elderflowers early in the day when it's sunny if you want that lovely floral aroma, not something that resembles cat's wee. If you have a Soda Stream you could give it some gas but I really like this without. It works equally well using some mint instead of lemon balm or just elderflower on its own. When serving this to friends, pretend the process was infinitely more complicated than it was, then sit back and accept the shower of compliments.

BLACK MUSTARD

Brassica nigra

Four-petalled bright
yellow flowers. The
flowering stem is often
branching

Narrow, upright seed
pods arranged around the
flowering stem

Rough to bristly crinkled
leaves with irregular
lobes. Tips becoming
more pointed towards
the flowers

PARTS USED: Leaves, flowers, seeds

HARVESTING TIP: Wear gloves if gathering large amounts – leaves can be rough on the hands

10th June. Somewhere east of the city

Every year, we all seem so shocked that it rains for most of June, but as anyone who has ever been to Glastonbury Festival will tell you, it absolutely chucks it down and this is the seasonal norm. Perhaps we are just such a positive bunch that we annually erase this small truth and replace it with soft-focus, childhood memories of endless hot summers. Today I ran a foraging event for a group of lovely people in an East End nature reserve, scheduled for a couple of hours, and despite the wet weather I ended up talking for nearly four hours straight, enthusing about the capital's wild plants and their myriad uses, touching, sniffing and tasting them as we went. An area of chalk soil, very unusual for London, produced plants I'm more used to seeing on a West Country clifftop than in the city, including the wonderful-looking and equally well-named viper's bugloss (go on, look it up) and a late patch of black mustard, which proved a big hit, most of its fiery-tasting leaves a bit wilted but still with hundreds of stunning little yellow flowers. Think cress meets mustard meets wasabi, a flavour bomb packed tightly into a delicate four-petalled flower, just waiting to explode on the top of a salad or soup.

After, rather tired but still keen to check out one patch we hadn't had time to visit, I found myself surrounded by the most enormous, almost tropical, stinging nettles and wondering, in true 'plant nerd' style, whether they were subspecies that produced such freakishly big leaves. I could talk for an hour about 'stingers', hence me mentioning them repeatedly in these pages, and so wonderful is this much neglected, wild superfood, with almost unlimited culinary uses, fantastic nutritional value and numerous medicinal applications, it really should be our national dish! So, what to do with these impressive-looking leaves? It struck me that they were the size of small dinner plates and then the answer became obvious . . . Tempura stinging nettle leaves, otherwise known as the Edible Dinner Plate, or at least a side plate big enough to serve a small salad on, eat the salad, then eat the plate. And what a success it was . . .

Stinging nettle tempura with a black mustard ponzu

For the tempura: *4–5 tbsp tempura batter mix, salt, cold sparkling water, oil, nettle leaves*

For the ponzu: *a good handful of black mustard flowers (or nasturtium leaves and petals), 2 tbsp soy sauce, ½ tbsp rice vinegar (or white wine vinegar), 1 tbsp lemon juice, 2–4 tsp caster sugar*

Tempura is a blend of plain flour and cornflour but I generally buy the ready-mixed version. Being something of a lazy cook, I always prefer the simplest option. I add a little salt to pep it up a bit and make it by combining the mix with some cold fizzy water, stirring with a fork to produce a thin, slightly bubbly batter. Too thin, add more mix; too thick, add more water. To fry the nettles go halfway between shallow- and deep-frying, putting about 5cm of oil into a shallow saucepan. When the oil is good and hot (test by dropping in a spot of batter), I carefully wipe one of my nettle leaves through the batter, turn it over and do the same again, then gently place it into the oil, being sure not to let it fold or wrinkle. It's the most fun part of the process and easy with a little practice, as is judging how much batter to use – too thick and the batter inflates, too thin and the nettle is too flimsy, just right and after about 1 minute you have the perfect edible plate.

For the ponzu use a handful of mustard flowers – nasturtium petals work well too – crushed and ground with a mortar and pestle until they form a yellow paste. In a small pan, gently warm the soy sauce with the rice vinegar (failing that, white wine vinegar) and the lemon juice. Now add between 2 and 4 teaspoons of caster sugar depending on how sweet you like it, and once dissolved stir in the mustard flower paste. Cool before serving. This is far from a traditional ponzu, which is much thinner and contains a fish and seaweed stock, but it's the wonderful mix of soy and lemon juice that I was after.

MARSH SAMPHIRE
Salicornia europaea

PARTS USED: Branching stem

Bright green segmented stems,
branching as it matures

SEA PLANTAIN
Plantago maritima

PARTS USED: Leaves

Lots of long narrow leaves

SEA PURSLANE

Atriplex portulacoides

PARTS USED: Leaves, flowers

The leaves are light grey/
green, elongated and
oval-shaped, with a mealy
coating

SEA ASTER

Aster tripolium

PARTS USED: Leaves

Pale purple petals
with a yellow
centre similar to
Michaelmas daisy

HARVESTING TIP: Be careful of sinking mud and
stay aware of the tides. Harvest the tender tops of all
these salt marsh plants, leaving any woody bits behind

13th June. I have escaped the city

The best place to learn *how* to forage is in the place you have easiest access to and are able to visit and revisit in all seasons, not just to pick things to eat but to become familiar with the plants you are interested in, at all stages of their development, learning to identify them when their most obvious features are on display and learning when to return to harvest them – often when only the tiniest details are visible. But, and this is quite a big but, to forage properly, we must learn to move around and there are numerous fantastic wild foods that just don't grow in the city . . . and I want to eat them! Dorset is one of my favourite places on Earth, allowing me to indulge my twin obsessions of rock climbing and foraging. Today was a non-climbing day and I spent it in one of the most fertile places I know, the southern end of Chesil Beach, a fantastic collision of different overlapping environments, where a fresh-water lagoon meets the sea. Salt water, brackish water, fresh water, sand, pebbles, chalky soil and wide salt marshes, all butted up against each other, making for something of a forager's paradise. My focus today was on the low tide and the salt marsh plants it reveals, the most well known of which is marsh samphire. Imagine an enormous mat of electric-green, spiky little fronds, like mini asparagus, stretching over hundreds of metres of the water's edge and its muddy flats. This carpet effect is common to most of these simple-to-identify, easy-to-pick plants and within half an hour I had all the ingredients I'd need for stir-fries, salads, fish cakes (minus the fish) and a host of other lovely dishes. Before I left this spot, and with ingredients found either right there or from a box I keep in the van, I knocked up some seasonal salt marsh pickles, an excellent way to enjoy these salty vegetables long after they have passed their prime.

Salt marsh pickles and salt marsh fish cakes

For the pickles: *various salt marsh vegetables, rice wine vinegar, brown sugar*

For the fish cakes: *cold mashed potato, smoked mackerel, onion, garlic cloves, marsh samphire, sea purslane, flour, salt and black pepper*

Gathered by the sea, washed quickly in fresh water, assembled in the van, photographed on the spot. The first two plants that went into my jar were sea purslane and marsh samphire (also known as glasswort), both in the 'wild spinach' family (a loose, not particularly botanical grouping). Like many coastal plants, they have modified themselves to become more succulent than their inland relatives and, as such, more resistant to the harsh coastal conditions, giving them a sweet, salty crunch, which makes them ideal for preserving. To these I added some sea aster (a relative of the daisy), some shrubby sea-blite (a plant described as 'nationally scarce but locally abundant'), sea plantain and, my absolute favourite, sea arrow grass, also known as coriander grass. I then added a 50:50 mix of rice wine vinegar and water and a few sachets of brown sugar that I 'borrowed' from the nearby cafe. Ready to eat in a matter of days, more a Japanese-style light pickle than a traditional English pickle-it-to-death type affair.

I am also very fond of using some of these salty plants to make fish cakes; the samphire tips and purslane leaves seem to work the best. I make burger-sized cakes by mixing cold mashed potatoes, flaked smoked mackerel, coarse ground black pepper and some finely chopped and fried onion and garlic. I stir in a handful or two of washed and chopped salt marsh plants and smoosh the whole lot together with my hands, then form them into cakes, dust in seasoned flour and fry until they are crispy and golden on both sides. Perfect with a dollop of my Hawthorn Relish (page 206) but just as tasty with good old tomato ketchup.

NASTURTIUM

Tropaeolum majus

The stems join the leaves towards the top and in the centre, from which white veins radiate

Flower colours vary from yellow to orange to red with a long 'nectar spur' at the base

Seeds are segmented into three with grooves running downwards

PARTS USED: Leaves, flowers, stems

HARVESTING TIP: The whole leaf stem is also good to eat when it's young

20th June. Crystal Palace

Today I visited Crystal Palace, one of my favourite areas south of the city. On entering the park I was immediately rewarded with some huge swathes of wild (possibly feral) rocket, with big tufts of grey-green leaves and bright yellow, four-petalled cabbage flowers that waved at me from hundreds of yards away. I was also stunned by how beautiful so many of the little front gardens in this area were; great to see that so much love had gone into such small spaces. When I got home, inspired by what I'd seen and more as a never to be repeated experiment than from a strong desire to eat what grows in the front gardens of my busy little London street, I wandered up one side and down the other to see what it would yield. If nothing else it was a nice snapshot of a few of the edible flowers that were in season. I knocked on everyone's door and explained what I was doing, receiving a generally enthusiastic response and one rather grumpy but totally justified 'leave my roses alone'.

Usually I pick wild flowers and wild leaves from patches of my local park that are well away from the road and where I have a good idea about the soil quality, but June in London is not the best time for most salad plants. Nature, however, is wonderfully perpetual, and as many of the leaves 'go over', out come the flowers. I can't overstress the need to correctly identify these; some of our most common flowers are also extremely toxic and eating them would make for a horrific experience, let alone a terrible salad. If you are not an experienced forager, a few edible varieties of domestic/garden flowers you may be able to easily identify are: rose, fuchsia, ox-eye daisy, day lily (illustrated overleaf) – not true lilies, be very careful not to eat any of those – courgette, borage, nasturtium (illustrated opposite), hibiscus, evening primrose and hollyhock. I should add that as with all new foods, a tolerance test is the best, if not the only approach to take. Don't just steam in and eat a plate full of something you have never tried before, regardless of whether it tastes nice. There's more about that in the chapter on safety (page 261).

DAY LILY
Hemerocallis fulva

Flowers are upward-facing with six orange 'petals' (called sepals) each with a paler orange stripe down the centre

Long, hairless leaf blades that taper gradually with a distinct ridge/keel on one side

Clusters of small fat tubers

PARTS USED: Leaves, shoots, flowers, young tubers

HARVESTING TIP: Avoid other day lily species unless you are sure they are edible and especially avoid any genuine lilies, which may be poisonous

Seasonal 'wild' flower salad

Whichever edible flowers you can lay your hands on, rose hip vinegar or sweet vinegar, light olive oil (optional)

For this salad I used a mixture of rose petals, lavender flowers, day lily pods and flowers (although I can find no record of this elsewhere, eating these sometimes gives me a sore throat . . . strange but true, so just have a small bite the first time you try them), linden (also known as lime) leaves, ox-eye daisy petals, fuchsia flowers (more for the look than the taste), wall bellflowers – a member of the Campanula/Bellflower family that grows all over London pretty much year round – and lastly some nasturtium flowers to give it a peppery bite. Before anyone misses the point, no, I'm not advocating that we all start 'scrumping' from our neighbours' gardens and I only took a flower from each, just the one time, OK? The key to making a wild salad, with flowers or leaves, is to allow various strong flavours to exist together, but in small amounts, in and amongst a larger quantity of one or two blander ingredients. In this mix the wall bellflowers and linden leaves are the 'base' ingredients, while the other flowers bring a variety of more intense flavours. I tend not to add any oil to flower salads, finding it a bit heavy on some of the more delicate petals, but a little wild rose vinegar (page 198), or a similarly gentle sweet vinegar, helps to bring all the flavours together, as I have mentioned before, enhancing the sweet tastes and 'taking the top off' the bitter ones. I make things like this all year long, even in winter when the joys of living in a microclimate provide me with salads and flowers that we more commonly associate with spring.

COMMON LIME/LINDEN
Tilia cordata

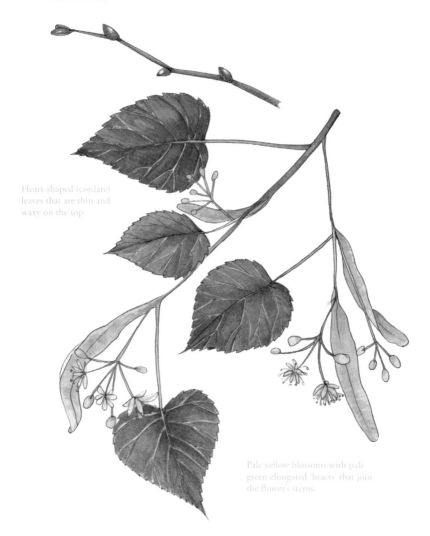

Heart-shaped (cordate)
leaves that are thin and
waxy on the top

Pale yellow blossoms with pale
green elongated 'bracts' that join
the flower's stems

PARTS USED: Young leaves, flowers (including bracts)

HARVESTING TIP: The young leaves should be translucent.
Pick the flowers with the bracts (looks like a thin leaf) still attached

27th June. Almost Regent's Park, but not quite

I'm often stunned at how green London is, for such a heavily populated, utterly massive city. We have so many green spaces to choose from that it's pretty much impossible to avoid them, unless you work in that place that bankers call 'the square mile', in which case there is almost no greenery and probably even less time to appreciate what little there is. I took my son to London Zoo today and after we left and went to get the car from the small but odiously priced car park over the road, I found myself, as I often do, checking out what was growing in this otherwise unassuming little spot.

'How often do you go foraging?' people sometimes ask me, but the question really misses the target. Whether picking something or not, when out and about I am *always* foraging, accumulating information and absorbing my surroundings in a way that takes no effort and is very similar to looking round a room full of people to see who I recognize. In about two minutes I counted eighteen different edible plants and eight fruiting or edible flowering trees. Daisies, nettles, mallow, three types of wild spinach, chickweed, rose hips, plum trees, rowan, linden, blackthorn. A mirror image of London, where every square inch is of value, here nature was abundant, compact but still thriving.

Foragers exist in a world of cusps and overlaps, constantly transitioning from one 'micro-season' to the next, and one of the sweetest of these is the point at which the last of the elderflowers are still out and the first of the lime/linden blossoms appear. Both have sweet scents but very different tastes; the latter reminds me of honeydew melon and the blossoms dry to make a sweet and calmative infusion, popular in France where it's known as *tilleul thé*. Lime blossom also makes amazing syrups, sorbets, all manner of wines and liqueurs, and I half knew what I had in mind when I hastily collected a carrier bag full: lime blossom champagne. I'm sure it's been made before but I haven't seen a recipe anywhere, so for now I will take the credit for this most wonderful, light and fizzy summer tipple.

Lime blossom champagne

600g granulated sugar, 1 lemon, 20 good handfuls of common lime blossom (or 20–30 elderflower sprays), 2 tbsp white wine vinegar, 1 tsp wine yeast

I made this by adapting the simplest and best of elderflower champagne recipes, from Roger Phillips's timeless classic *Wild Food*, substituting a large handful of lime blossoms for every elderflower spray. This really is a great summer drink and ideal to make as the elderflower disappears and the lime blossom is still at its best. Add the sugar to 1 gallon, that's 4.5 litres, of water, and warm gently until it dissolves (better still, dissolve the sugar in much less water then add the rest cold). Next, squeeze in the juice of the lemon, quarter the squeezed lemon and throw it in too, then pour the lot into a large sterilized bucket or big container (sluice with boiling water, ideally adding a sterilizing powder specifically for brewing). Add the blossoms and white wine vinegar and give it a good stir. At this stage, you can cover the container with muslin or a thin clean cloth and leave it for 5–7 days while nature and airborne 'wild' yeasts do their work, although I usually add a little wine yeast to give it a bit of a head start, but make sure the liquid is no hotter than tepid (40°C) or it will kill the yeast. After this initial fermentation, strain the liquid through muslin, no need to siphon it out as you would with a beer, and put into sterilized screw- or swing-top bottles. It will be ready to drink in about another week but tastes better, slightly drier and fuller flavoured after 2–3 weeks. A generally more sophisticated summer drink than elderflower champagne, at least I think so – but then I would, wouldn't I?

July

Comfrey fritters and a ribwort 'seaweed' salad

Wild rocket hummus

Mugwort and ox-eye daisy mead

Wild spinach aloo

Pineapple weed granita

'As foragers we become acutely aware of the changes in season as well as the plants that grow around us; this intimacy gives people a deep empathy with their local green spaces, as even the grottiest spot of waste ground becomes a cherished friend if it plays host to a delicious wild crop . . .'

RIBWORT PLANTAIN

Plantago lanceolata

The black, oval-shaped heads
have white/yellowish flowers
growing outwards. There are no
leaves on the flower stems

The leaves are
long and narrow
with vertical veins
that can pull out
like threads when
snapped. Slightly
waxy in texture

The flower heads become
longer and dry, producing
numerous brown seeds

PARTS USED: Leaves, flowers, seeds

HARVESTING TIP: Younger leaves are less stringy than the older ones. Seed heads taste like
mushrooms when they are still black, then more like cereal grain when they turn brown

2nd July. Victoria Park

It was the start of July and I had just been for a stroll around Victoria Park. I like to pretend that what I do is real work so I'd decided that this trip was some early preparation for a walk I was running there in the autumn. According to the council's website, this was the first East End park to be created, after a mass petition was sent to Queen Victoria in 1840 asking her for a green space to improve the quality of life for the 400,000 people living in local slums. As the first public park to be specifically built for London's working-class residents, it became known as 'the people's park', and the west lake, around which I do lots of my foraging, was originally called 'the bathing pond', a massive communal washing facility. Today there were people fishing and boating but no one taking a dip. Although the sun was hot and the water looked tempting, bathing is no longer allowed – a shame if you ask me. For obvious reasons, my life couldn't be more different from that of a late Victorian 'East Ender' but it's clear that our parks still serve a similar purpose, providing a place to play and relax, a cleansing environment in an otherwise frantic, work-orientated city. Without these green spaces I would be unable to tolerate living here at all.

I only walked for an hour but came across about forty edible and medicinal plants, the majority of them bordering the lake and some, like the big patch of reedmace (bulrush) I spotted, growing in it. At the top of today's picking list were just two plants: common comfrey, which thrives on the water's edge, covered with large bristly leaves and bunches of white 'bellflowers'; and the much smaller ribwort plantain, which grows utterly everywhere. Comfrey is used widely in herbal medicine, contains generous amounts of beta-carotene, vitamin B2, potassium and manganese, and, as its old name 'knitbone' suggests, it acts as a cell proliferant, i.e. it helps cells to regrow. Today, I picked just two dozen leaves; my interest was in making fritters rather than herbal remedies.

Ribwort plantain also has numerous medicinal uses, most notably as a 'drawing herb', containing polysaccharides that attract fluid and make it excellent at removing toxins or foreign substances from the body. I have used it often for getting hard-to-grab splinters to come to the surface and also to remove a tiny bit of glass from my wife's foot, chewing its leaves to make a 'spit poultice', securing it with a plaster and leaving it on overnight to do its work. I gathered about a hundred of these long thin leaves with something of a culinary experiment in mind, and also bagged a few dozen seed heads. Resembling tiny microphones, they taste of mushroom when fresh, and dry to make an excellent, fibre-rich topping for cereals. Then it was off home to play.

Comfrey fritters and a ribwort 'seaweed' salad

There are various species of comfrey, many of which contain alkaloids that may (or may not) be harmful to the liver, *if* they are consumed in quantity and over a long period of time. Although no conclusive evidence actually exists, there still remains a question mark over the long-term effects of heavy consumption of this group of plants. Common comfrey (*Symphytum officinale*), however, has a long and happy history as an edible plant, eaten all over Europe, and having looked into this topic at much greater length than discussed here, I'd suggest that eating fritters made from its leaves a couple of times a year is absolutely fine. Do bear in mind that all things are potentially dangerous if consumed in large enough quantities, even water!

For the 'seaweed' salad: *ribwort leaves, cucumber, soy sauce, brown rice vinegar, sesame oil, furikake sprinkles*

For the fritters: *100g self-raising flour, 100ml chilled soda water or beer, 1 egg white, oil, common comfrey leaves, salt and pepper*

I must admit that until I read an inspiring article from Transitional Gastronomy, two wild food obsessives based in LA, I had written off ribwort leaves as something of a 'survival' food, too tough and not enough flavour to bother with. These clever Americans had been experimenting with different cooking times and temperatures for these, and many other, not so edible leaves, and claimed that not only had they found ribwort to be very tasty, if cooked for just the right duration it became tender, too. With a big pan of salted boiling water and a sink full of cold, I set about running my own experiment, finding that there is indeed a point at which the leaves stop being tough, and just before they get too saturated, they become soft and gelatinous. Obviously it will depend on the size and age of the leaves used, but I found a point at roughly 3½ minutes was perfect, whipping them out of the pan and straight into the sink full of cold water to stop the cooking. Timing is crucial, though; five seconds too late and you have mush, just ten seconds early and they are too tough.

These tender, slightly slimy leaves really reminded me of seaweed so I mixed them with chopped cucumber and dressed them with soy, rice wine vinegar, sesame oil and Japanese furikake sprinkles. My first central London seaweed salad was a roaring success, but it needed something hot to serve with it.

This recipe is for a simple traditional fritter batter which can be used with other green leafy plants, too, providing they are robust enough to survive in hot oil for a couple of minutes.

Mix the flour with the soda water or beer; it's very important that this is chilled. Add salt and pepper, then whisk the egg white and add it to the mixture (although opinion is divided on this ingredient: some people add the whole egg, others leave it out completely). Put the batter in the fridge while heating a pan with 8–10cm oil to about 180°C. If, like me, testing the temperature is just too specific, check the oil sizzles when a tiny spot of batter is dropped into it. Give the batter a quick stir before adding the leaves, then one at a time drop them into the oil, frying for 1 minute on each side before quickly draining on kitchen paper and serving hot.

WILD ROCKET
(PERRENIAL WALL ROCKET)
Diplotaxis tenuifolia

Four-petalled bright
yellow flowers

Narrow leaves with
deep, irregular lobes

Upright seed
pods branch
out from the
main stem

PARTS USED: Leaves, flowers

HARVESTING TIP: If it's flowering, pull the leaves
away from the stem, which is usually too tough to eat

MUGWORT
Artemisia vulgaris

Petals are barely visible.
Flower heads are strongly
aromatic when rubbed

The leaf underside
has furry white
hairs and is much
paler than the
topside

PARTS USED: Leaves, flowers

HARVESTING TIP: There is still plenty of flavour in the flowering tops of the dead plants,
which are useful for seasoning and brewing

14th July. The Waterworks Nature Reserve

This fascinating and wild corner of Leyton was once known as the Essex Filter Beds, a complex network of wetlands, trenches and tunnels, built in 1850 to provide the surrounding areas with a much needed freshwater supply. The six original beds were enormous constructions, formed around a central well and bordered with trees, so I imagine it was also quite a picturesque spot in its day despite its practical function. Today the landscape is very different but plenty of evidence of its history is visible, a couple of the original beds forming lakes which make up the heart of this nature reserve. After many emails and a few long telephone conversations, I was able to convince the powers that be to let me run a wild food walk here, explaining that the events I organize are focused on learning about wild plants, not on gathering huge armfuls of whatever we come across. This has been one of the biggest challenges for me, creating good relationships with the various governing bodies of the land on which I run most of my events, although mostly they have been very receptive when I explain how foraging and interacting with the landscape actually promotes ecological stewardship rather than the reverse. As foragers we become acutely aware of the changes in season as well as the plants that grow around us; this intimacy gives people a deep empathy with their local green spaces, as even the grottiest patch of waste ground becomes a cherished friend if it plays host to a delicious wild crop.

Today's walk was a freebie for a London-based foraging group, and unlike most of my walks, quite a few of the participants already had a good basic knowledge of wild plants. Fortunately I was able to show them a few that they had never seen before, starting with a big patch of field pepperwort, a lovely 'cressy' member of the Cabbage family, with crunchy leaves topped with towers of peppery white flowers. Around a small pond we picked some water mint and then looked at the differences between edible reedmace and its mildly toxic lookalike, yellow flag iris. As we walked, numerous other plants were rubbed, sniffed, touched and tasted until we hit upon a small area of meadow and, with it, thousands of ox-eye daisies. Much like our common lawn daisy, these have yellow and white flower heads, although much bigger, they grow up to 3 inches across and the plants themselves can stand a couple of feet tall. The flowers and leaves are both edible and have a sweetly perfumed taste that reminds me of bubblegum. I like to include the leaves in salads, often finding them growing throughout the winter, and today it was fun to get the group munching the flower heads straight off the stems – just one per person, though. I picked a few for my own bag and we moved on to look at some mugwort, another member of the Daisy family but a very different creature indeed, with historical uses including everything from beer-making to promoting 'lucid dreaming'.

Mugwort is a fascinating herb, with a smell reminiscent of rosemary and distinctive dark green leaves with very pale undersides. I find smells to be so evocative that more often than not I just let the plants do the thinking for me, so standing there with this group, all of us rubbing and smelling this plant's wonderful aroma, the idea of creating a mugwort and ox-eye daisy mead just popped into my head.

Mugwort and ox-eye daisy mead

Mugwort is such a versatile plant and I am constantly learning new ways to use it, most recently adding a few spoons of powdered dried leaves and flowers to a mushroom soup, only to discover its amazing powers as a flavour enhancer. Without doubt, it helped create the most 'mushroomy' mushroom soup I have ever tasted, and it will also make a great accompaniment to roast lamb, the blend of sweetness and slight bitterness making it ideal to take the place of rosemary.

Organic honey, mineral water, a fistful of mugwort leaves and flowers and another of ox-eye daisy flowers, a pinch of brewer's yeast

Making mead is fun, simple and very rewarding. I'm no expert but that has never stopped me. I recently made a wonderfully fruity elderflower and cherry mead; to be specific this should be referred to as a melomel not a mead, it containing fruit not just herbs. For my mugwort and ox-eye daisy mead I used a ratio of one part organic honey to four parts of mineral water, combining them to three-quarters fill a large kilner jar. Then in went a decent-sized fistful of both plants and a pinch of brewer's yeast to help it along, although if you prefer it's possible to omit this and just allow natural airborne yeast to get the fermentation going. If you do choose the 'nature's own yeasts' method, you may need to re-boost the fermentation process after a week or two with the addition of some extra honey. Every day I gave the liquid a good stir with a chopstick, spinning it round for thirty seconds or so and after about a week it had become frothy as the yeast began to do its work. Four weeks at room temperature and a daily dose of cyclonic stirring later, and I had produced an extraordinary-tasting drink, which I strained through muslin to remove the plant matter. It should have then been bottled but mine just lived in the jar in the fridge.

I can't quite describe the taste – it's sweet and also intensely aromatic, but each time I have a glass I feel like sitting cross-legged on the grass and listening to early Pink Floyd albums . . . What does it all mean, man? Mead is such an easy drink to play with, strong-flavoured plants work very well and I'd recommend trying all sorts of versions, using a mix of plants, fruit and flowers. What have you got to lose except your inhibitions?

FAT HEN
Chenopodium album

PARTS USED: Leaves, seeds

Mealy texture on the leaves

GOOD KING HENRY
Blitum bonus-henricus

PARTS USED: Leaves, young stems

Pointed lobes at the
base of the leaves

SPEAR-LEAVED
ORACHE
Atriplex prostrata

PARTS USED: Leaves, young stems

Arrow-shaped leaves, with
irregularly ridged to smooth edges

HARVESTING TIP: Pull the tops of large bunches together to cut them off all in one go

20th July. Ravenscourt Park

Come high summer – if ever English summertime could be credited with such a thing – the majority of the plants I forage for earlier in the year have become too bitter, woody or just generally too tough to use. At this time of year the seashore is probably a better location for foraging than the city, but as the salads and spring greens dry out, they are replaced with new crops, summer flowers and early fruits. Ravenscourt Park is a terrific place, not just for foraging but for learning about it, too, with so many of the plants I like to eat being very easy to identify in mid-summer. Even if they are well past their best in terms of flavour and texture, all the key ID features are on show: flowers, seeds, mature leaves, basically the information needed to become confident with a plant's identity and providing a solid basis on which to return the following spring when there is far less on show but the plants are at their most edible.

Today I was rewarded with a small bag of intensely sweet cherry plums, some deep purple damsons and the dried seed heads from about a hundred broadleaf plantain stems. Just a teaspoon of these contains as much fibre as an entire bowl of porridge, no disrespect to the Scots – in fact it was eminent Scottish herbalist Monica Wilde who first introduced me to the similarities between this plant and the closely related but pricey psyllium husk sold in health food shops. In the middle of the park there had obviously been some refurbishment work, new walls built and paths widened. A recently removed 'portacabin', presumably the site office for these works, had left behind a huge rectangular footprint, where nothing had been able to grow for months. Now uncovered, not only had this space filled up with numerous opportunistic wild plants, prepared to set seed at a moment's notice, the entire area was ring fenced with wooden stakes making it inaccessible to dogs and ideal for me. Among the stinging nettles and poisonous plants like woody nightshade, a relative of deadly nightshade, I was able to pick five separate varieties of wild spinach, which conveniently begin to appear in early June as many of the other 'forageable' greens become inedible. Relatives of spinach, these plants included some with wonderful names, like Good King Henry, fig-leaved goosefoot, spear-leaved orache and fat hen. Although their leaves come in a variety of weird and wonderful shapes, tastewise they are all relatively similar. With the hot weather and all this wild spinach . . . I felt a curry coming on.

Wild spinach aloo

I tend to use all the varieties of wild spinach that I collect, and also the unrelated but equally tasty stinging nettle, in much the same way. I sweat or steam them as a green veg, use them in soups, stews, smoothies and omelettes, mix them with lentil dhal or bake them with pasta and cheese. Basically the list of uses for these plants is endless, but like a good organic spinach, I find them a little bitter and slightly soapy-tasting before they've been cooked. As a result I rarely use them in salads, with young sea beet leaves as the only exception to this; they taste more like ready-salted snacks so I find them irresistible.

This recipe is for a basic but delicious spinach and potato curry that could easily include other ingredients; the potatoes could be replaced with chickpeas or omitted entirely.

4 medium potatoes, ½ tsp each garam masala, ground cumin, turmeric and coriander, 2 tbsp lemon juice, 1 tsp salt, 1 tsp brown sugar, oil, 2 medium-hot green chillies, 1 onion, 1 tsp black mustard seeds, 1 tsp cumin seeds, 2 tomatoes, 400g wild spinach

Serves 2–3

First peel the potatoes and chop them each into about eight pieces. Now mix together the garam masala, cumin, turmeric and coriander. Roll the potatoes in the spices and add the lemon juice, 2 tablespoons of water, the salt and sugar. If you have time, leave the mixture to sit for 20 minutes or so.

Heat some oil in a frying pan, remove the potatoes from the spice mixture and cook for about 15 minutes, stirring them regularly until they are golden brown. Remove the potatoes and in the same pan, add more oil and fry the green chillies (chopped and deseeded) together with a finely diced onion and the mustard and cumin seeds. Finely chop the tomatoes, return the potatoes to the pan, adding the remainder of the spice mixture with the finely chopped tomatoes and more oil if needed. Allow it to reduce a little before roughly chopping the spinach and adding a bunch at a time until it's all wilted. Reduce the heat to minimum, cover and cook for an additional 5–10 minutes, depending on how long you can wait. Serve with steamed rice or Indian bread and plain yogurt.

PINEAPPLE WEED

Matricaria discoidea

Looks like a chamomile flower that has
lost its petals. Smells like pineapple

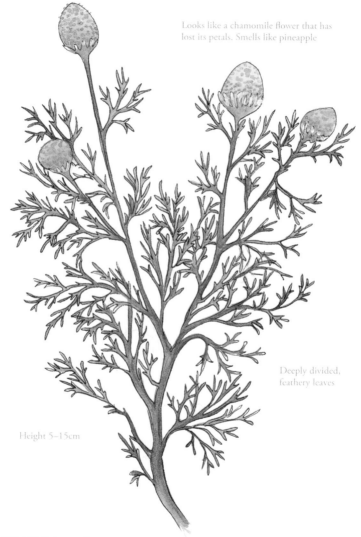

Deeply divided,
feathery leaves

Height 5–15cm

PARTS USED: Leaves, flowers
HARVESTING TIP: Cut off just the top quarter of the plant, including the flowers

30th July. Finsbury Park

Pineapple weed is a close relative of chamomile and, like so many of the plants we resentfully describe as invasive, it was brought into the UK by British botanists. It was originally introduced in 1781 and ninety years later escaped from Kew Gardens. Deciding that it liked it here so much, it hasn't looked back since. Other common names like wild chamomile or disc mayweed just don't do justice to this wonderful little plant which thoroughly deserves its name, looking, smelling and tasting as it does, like pineapple. Today I visited Finsbury Park, on something of a hit and run mission, more specifically to use the running track, having actually convinced myself that I would be moving too fast and puffing too hard to see anything edible, let alone stop to pick it. It was a sweltering day, such a contrast to the times I'd spent here in the winter, shivering my arse off in the windswept playground, while my son made sandcastles. I'm not tremendously enthusiastic about exercise (except rock climbing, which doesn't count) and I'd been running since I left home, so by the time I got to the track I was in full flight, already breathing hard, trying to keep my focus on the task in hand and not let my attention, and my enthusiasm, wander. I find the best way to do this when I run is to stare at the ground in front of me and as a result I have developed a quite odd style, with both hands lolloping at my sides and my head dropping over – the missing link, out for a jog. It serves me well, though, and usually acts as a quite effective set of anti-foraging blinkers, especially on a properly managed track that, as you'd expect, is unlikely to yield much in the way of wild food.

Not so today; as I ran, little flashes of yellow and green kept popping into view, blurring and whizzing off behind me. I knew instantly what they were, I was just a little surprised to find them right here. Chefs and bartenders are quite excited by the prospect of using pineapple weed these days and I get a few calls a year asking where they can find some. My usual response is to direct them to the grottiest bit of ground they know, preferably a well-trodden and bare-looking spot in the middle of a park or patch of waste ground, just the sort of places that pineapple weed thrives in. I completed my last lap before I stopped – honestly I did – then set about doing my bit for the community and the thankless task of clearing the track of this 'nasty invasive weed' (delicious edible treat), filling my pockets and my hands with its flowers and leaving the rest of the foliage behind in the grass.

Pineapple weed granita

Because this plant tastes of pineapple it has many different uses, most of which I have not got round to trying yet. My friend and author of the great book *Booze For Free*, Andy Hamilton, reliably informs me that pineapple weed steeped in rum with gorse flowers makes a good basis for a tropical-tasting daiquiri made only with UK-growing plants. Yorkshireman and forager Craig Worrell uses his local crop to make sorbets and cordials and Mark Williams in Scotland mixes his with honey and sweet cicely to make a delicious mead.

250–300g pineapple weed flowers, 250g sugar, small pinch of salt, juice of 1 lemon, vodka

This traditional Sicilian dessert is served semi-frozen, a similar dish but coarser than a sorbet and incorporating a variety of fruit and fresh herbs including oranges, strawberries, mint, lemon, jasmine and black mulberries. Pineapple weed seemed like the obvious wild ingredient to use in mine.

Gently heat the pineapple weed flowers in 500ml water and leave to infuse for 12–24 hours. Strain and discard the flowers, adding the sugar to the water and warming until it dissolves. Add the salt, lemon juice and a capful of vodka before cooling the mixture in the fridge for an hour, at the same time putting an empty, shallow-sided metal dish in the freezer. After an hour, pour the chilled liquid into the metal dish and replace it in the freezer, returning every 30–60 minutes to stir the crystals that form around the edge back into the centre. Repeat this process for 3–4 hours until the texture is coarse but still slightly slushy. If you're feeling creative, you might try candying the discarded flower heads by adapting November's recipe for candied quince (page 223).

August

Meadowsweet cordial

Classic rose hip syrup and rose hip and chilli sauce

Wild masala chai

Black and white mulberry mess

Hazelnut pancakes with a wild flower syrup

'I saw the wonderful purple stains all over the pavement before
I got close enough to see if the fruit was ripe, then carefully
climbed into the centre of "my" tree, to very delicately remove
a few dozen of its delicious fruits, most of which came home in
my bag, the rest already in my belly . . .'

MEADOWSWEET

Filipendula ulmaria

Pairs of toothed
leaflets with tiny
leaflets in between

The stems and leaf stalks
are often red to reddish-
green

Five-petalled white to creamy
white flowers are borne in clusters
on branching flower heads

PARTS USED: Flowers, young leaves

HARVESTING TIP: Leave the flowers outside to allow insects to crawl or fly away. While the
flowers taste of almond or marzipan, the young leaves have a distinct cucumber/melon flavour,
but should be used sparingly due to the presence of salacin, which is used to make aspirin

1st August. Holland Park

Well I never expected that. Probably because of its location in one of London's most expensive postcodes, I had always assumed that Holland Park would be a mirror image of the neighbourhood that surrounds it, exclusive and anything but welcoming to the urban forager. How wrong I was. Not only does it have some large wild areas, rambling nature reserves where the flora and fauna are left to their own devices, it also has an amazing array of fruit and nut trees and a couple of small, comparatively unmanaged lakes, at least in terms of the plant life that surrounds them. From a mature common walnut tree close to the cafe, I collected a couple of dozen large green nuts, with an idea to make a *nocino*, a traditional Italian liqueur, bittersweet and made with unripe walnuts flavoured with cinnamon, cloves and vanilla.

On an avenue of tall lime trees, their leaves now too robust for a salad and their blossoms long gone, I spotted a rather scruffy little tree with rutted dark grey bark and dull green oval leaves. As if it had been decorated for an out of season joke, it was covered with bright red and yellow orbs; fortunately for me they were cherry plums, not tacky Christmas baubles. There are a million culinary uses for these amazing little fruits, being as they are somewhere between a cherry and a plum, although my most common preparation for consumption involves nothing more complicated than a rinse under the tap.

A few dozen made it into my bag, but twenty or thirty of these got eaten as I wandered around, finally arriving at one of the small lakes and finding it garlanded with fluffy white flowers, many-headed feather dusters smelling of almond oil and vanilla. Meadowsweet likes wet places – riverbanks, ditches or sodden ground – and here it was, in full flower and forming a stunning perimeter to this small body of water. Not wishing to disrupt this idyllic scene, I gently nipped off just one flower head every few metres, filling a small bag but leaving no trace of my activity. Meadowsweet cordial may be one of the most common foraged drinks, but if made properly it really is the taste of summertime.

Meadowsweet cordial

My lovely friend Amy first introduced me to this recipe. Meadowsweet in full bloom makes for a stunning sight on a sunny riverside, with its white candyfloss flowers and wonderful aroma. Drunk as a cordial it has an almondy sweetness but needs preparing correctly to get the best out of it.

400g sugar, juice of 1 lemon, about 50 meadowsweet flower heads

Dissolve the sugar in 2 litres of nearly boiling water (you can use less but I find this just about right) and let it cool before adding the lemon juice. Then add the meadowsweet flower heads and warm very gently for about 10 minutes before leaving the liquid to cool again and infuse for 24 hours. Be sure not to overheat it, or the resulting cordial will be a little bitter and taste rather medicinal. Just like willow bark, meadowsweet contains a glucoside called salicin, from which we get salicylic acid, more commonly known as aspirin. This can give the cordial an unusual back taste if prepared without due care, so ignore any recipes that recommend boiling or overheating these delicate little flowers and you will produce what I consider to be a truly delicious drink. Strain out the flowers through muslin or a fine sieve and store the liquid in sterilized bottles.

Opinion is divided and I have had comments ranging from 'delicious mixed with gin' to 'this tastes like washing-up liquid', but for me this drink tastes its best just served with freezing cold fizzy water. I'd also suggest trying meadowsweet instead of lime blossom or elderflower in a wild-flower champagne, as on page 122. You could also make an almondy liqueur by infusing it with brandy and sugar, or adapt my pineapple weed granita (page 141) or water mint ice cream (page 101) recipes.

JAPANESE ROSE

Rosa rugosa

The leaves are symetrically
divided into 5–7 leaflets with
a rough feel to them

Flowers have five wide,
overlapping, pink petals with
many stamens

The fruit (hips) are short, round
and red with five long drooping
appendages (called sepals)

PARTS USED: Flowers, fruit

HARVESTING TIP: Timing is key, so avoid underripe or overripe (sloppy) fruit

14th August. A community garden in Dalston

One of the loveliest aspects of my job, if I can stretch the truth far enough to actually call it that, is being invited to places I would never otherwise go to. In the past year that would include a stately home, a city zoo, a gin distillery, a wild and wonderful Scottish island and various private houses and gardens. Today I visited a community growing project, hidden behind a church on the cusp of east and north London, a city gardener's paradise bursting with vegetable beds and tended by a bunch of very knowledgeable horticulture enthusiasts. I'm always slightly daunted by people who use too much Latin and, although it's not been through choice, I have had to learn many of the plant names that gardeners commonly refer to. Sometimes this has been useful to help me identify specific plants, on other occasions, as the police would say, 'to eliminate them from my enquiries'. To explore the world of edible plants is also to explore the world of the inedible and poisonous, many of which crop up in people's gardens. Fortunately, today's group were not interested in showing off their prowess with a dead language and were far keener to identify some of the wild plants that grow between their vegetable beds. As a result we all got on famously and were able to share our knowledge, me learning a few good growing tips and them getting to discover the delights of chickweed, hedge mustard, ground elder, nipplewort and sow thistle.

In the middle of roughly thirty raised beds and forming the centrepiece to this amazing little plot of land, stood a circular hedge, more of a thicket than anything, but definitely an intentional addition. A mix of bramble, dogwood and blackthorn intertwined and intermingled to create an impenetrable wildlife sanctuary, the outside of which was covered in great big Japanese rose hips, nearer the size of ping-pong balls than our more modest native varieties. We hadn't discussed a fee for my time but I was more than happy to pick a bag of these as my payment.

Classic rose hip syrup and rose hip and chilli sauce

For the syrup: *1kg rose hips, 500g white sugar*

For the sauce: *500ml rose hip syrup, 1 tsp chilli powder, 1 tsp turmeric powder, gravy powder*

I find Japanese rose hips more enjoyable to cook with than most of our native species; they are much bigger and become ripe in mid-August, but any variety, wild or otherwise, will do perfectly well for this recipe and different types will give varying flavours.

Bring the hips and about 1.5 litres of water to the boil and simmer for 20 minutes. While they are cooking, smash them up with a potato masher, before straining into a large clean bowl, using a sieve lined with a double layer of muslin (important it's doubled to avoid any of the fine hairs from the centre of the hip getting into the mix). Either wait for it to cool down a bit or get your rubber gloves on, twisting the muslin with the fruit inside into a ball and squeezing out every last drop of the liquid. Take the squashed fruit that's left inside the muslin, return it to the pan, add another 1.5 litres of water and repeat the process before mixing both sets of strained liquid together. At this point, many rose hip syrup recipes recommend adding literally kilos of sugar, hailing from a time before refrigeration, more specifically before the invention of the freezer, when they would have required it as a preservative. This just isn't necessary anymore and I would suggest adding just 500g of sugar, heating the liquid until it dissolves. Taste it and you will be delighted to discover that without the addition of masses of sweetness, you have a sauce that tastes of mango, papaya and tomato, tropical flavours we don't usually expect from plants and fruit in the UK. If you want more sugar, add it, then bottle some in sterilized glass bottles for the fridge and the rest in plastic bottles for the freezer. It keeps forever, or I assume it does as mine never sticks around for long.

If you'd prefer your syrup to become a cordial, to dilute later with fizzy water, you will need to add plenty of sugar to it, almost as much as there is liquid.

For a spicy, fruity sauce to serve with meat, blend 500ml rose hip syrup with the chilli powder, turmeric powder and any other spices you fancy. Reduce in a saucepan for 3–4 minutes and blend with a little gravy powder.

ALEXANDERS
Smyrnium olusatrum

PARTS USED: Leaves, young
stems, flowers, seeds

Black ridged seeds with
a strong black pepper
smell when crushed

WILD MARJORAM
Origanum vulgare

PARTS USED: Leaves with flowers

Pale lilac flowers clasped by a reddish-purple base

HARVESTING TIP: Be 100 per cent sure of your ID. Collecting and drying fresh plants
makes them much easier to identify, although this is not possible with most seeds

SWEET WOODRUFF
Galium odoratum

PARTS USED: Leaves, flowers, stems

Leaves appear in a wheel
(called a whorl) in a circle
round the stem, looking like an
Elizabethan ruff

White flowers emerge
from red-tipped buds

WATER PEPPER
Persicaria hydropiper

PARTS USED: Leaves with flowers

HARVESTING TIP: Be 100 per cent sure of your ID. It makes more sense to collect fresh
plants and dry them, although this is not possible with most seeds

15th August. Clapham Common

Today I ran a private event, a foraging walk for a swanky south London cocktail bar, an excitable bunch, brimming with ideas and eager to explore and utilize some of the city's wild flavours in their drinks. It was a roasting hot day and many of the plants we encountered were very dried out, still useful in many ways but not looking their best. After we parted company it occurred to me that this was an excellent opportunity to forage for a few ingredients for my 'dry store'. Like everyone else, I use a selection of spices to cook with: Asian flavours like chilli and cumin and aromatic European herbs like basil and thyme. Unlike most people, though, my dried spice collection contains numerous 'wild' plants and seeds, dried mushrooms and seaweeds, many of which are almost unheard of in contemporary cooking, ingredients like clove root, pepper dulse, magnolia, water pepper, crow garlic, alexanders, sweet woodruff, hogweed, peppery bolete and hoary mustard. Our 'neglected native spice rack' is a place of wonder for me, an array of fascinating flavours, many of which would have been commonplace in the UK before the arrival of more exotic spices in the late 1400s rendered them obsolete, or at least unfashionable. I could add another fifty to this ever-expanding list which allows me to constantly experiment with wild foods all year round, not just when specific things are in season.

Despite its wealthy, well-groomed location, Clapham Common has some lovely wild patches, so armed with some plastic resealable bags I was able to collect enough wild marjoram to last me for the rest of the year, as well as some alexanders seeds to use as a pepper substitute, aromatic hogweed seeds for baking and flavouring drinks, some spearmint and some wild plums that were too tasty to even make it home. The strong sunshine and the heady smells of these lovely native spices put me in mind of my last trip to India, punctuated by long train journeys and cups of sweet spicy chai. With the enthusiasm for flavour shown by my would-be wild cocktail makers, I wondered if I could make a native wild chai and headed home to raid my spice cupboard and get experimenting.

Wild masala chai

I am always fascinated to explore our local equivalents to some of the world's more exotic spices, and this is what led me last year to create a twenty-one-ingredient, native jerk seasoning for chicken or fish, but that, as they say, is another story, and a very long one, too.

Conventional chai: 5cm cube of ginger root, 2 tsp black peppercorns, 12 cloves, 8 cardamom pods, 5cm length vanilla pod, 5cm length cinnamon stick, 300ml whole milk, 2 tsp black tea, 2 tsp honey

Wild chai: a dozen dried magnolia petals, alexanders seeds, hogweed seeds, clove root, sweet woodruff, 2 tsp honey, 300ml whole milk, 2 tsp roasted and ground dandelion root, lavender flowers, fennel seeds, bog myrtle

For my wild chai, I started by making a conventional version, partly to see if mine came up to scratch and also to help me create a comparable drink.

For the traditional blend, I used 300ml water and added the sliced cube of ginger, the peppercorns, cloves, cardamom and vanilla pods and cinnamon stick, then brought it to the boil and simmered for 5 minutes. Then I added the whole milk, black tea and honey and simmered gently for another 5 minutes before straining. Perfect – India in a teacup.

Now for my wild creation, and I should stress you don't need every one of these foraged plants, you could just make a normal chai and substitute one or two ingredients or experiment with whatever you have – masala means a mix, so mix it up, play and see what you come up with. Instead of ginger I used a dozen dried magnolia petals, which have a strong chicory meets ginger taste to them, and instead of black pepper I substituted alexanders seeds but used only 1 teaspoon – they are so much stronger than pepper and have a bitter back taste. The cinnamon stick was replaced with a teaspoon of hogweed seeds and the cloves with half a dozen strands of wood avens (aka clove root), which has a taste like a mix of clove and nutmeg. For the vanilla I used a wonderfully aromatic

Black and white mulberry mess

Imagine large blackberries, elongated to twice their normal length, pinned all over the most twisted and dishevelled of trees and partially hidden under large green serrated leaves. Add to this the dripping juice, blood red and able to make a forager's hands look more like those of a mass murderer, that or Lady Macbeth, and you have a very accurate picture of the black mulberry, one of my all-time favourite fruits and something I look forward to all year. This recipe may be a great showcase for these amazing-tasting fruits but, to be honest, I usually just eat all of mine on the way home from the park. I wouldn't really call it a recipe; it's more a guide to assembly, using just a few fabulously tasty ingredients, all tossed in together. I managed to gather a decent quantity of mixed mulberries and although I'd happily make this with just the black ones, I'd probably not do so with just the white . . . Failing that, I'd use whatever wild fruits I could find and mix them up with strawberries and raspberries.

500ml double cream, 1 tbsp caster sugar, 4–5 ready-made meringue 'nests', 500g black and white mulberries, mint

Serves 4–6

Gently whip the cream with the caster sugar, just enough for it to stiffen a little, before breaking up the meringue 'nests' and folding them together with the cream. Wash the mulberries (or mixed fruits) and put them in a bowl, carefully squashing them to release some juice. With black mulberries this is hardly necessary, as they will already be dripping everywhere. Now mix the fruit and juice into the cream and meringue and serve decorated with extra fruit and chopped mint.

If ever you're faced with a glut of these amazing fruits (oh, lucky you!) consider making a black mulberry compote by cooking them for 3–5 minutes with a little water, sugar and a vanilla pod.

HAZEL
Corylus avellana

Nuts clasped in cases with pointed teeth, both starting off green and turning brown

Alternate and finely toothed leaves with pointed tips

Pale yellow male catkins, 3–10cm long, appear before leaves

PARTS USED: Nuts

HARVESTING TIP: Pick the nuts when they are almost ripe but still green, and before the grey squirrels get to them

30th August. Cody Dock, where the River Thames meets the River Lea

Today, with a million plus people heading to west London for Notting Hill Carnival, I found myself drawn in the opposite direction. I cycled to Victoria Park but, fuelled with coffee and sunshine, I didn't stop to look around. Instead I headed to the junction of the Thames and the much smaller River Lea, which starts life in the Chiltern Hills and winds south through the city until the two rivers meet, just below Cody Dock. I first discovered this place when I was asked to run a community walk here last year. Hidden behind some rather grotty-looking warehouses, this former industrial dock was abandoned for many years and remained neglected while all around it the East End was redeveloped. More recently, with a mixture of funding from the National Lottery and various other sources, it's been reopened and now has a riverside cafe, artists' workshops, studios and live/work spaces.

I wandered along the Lea, finding a few types of wild spinach that thrive in the summer months, then a patch of common mallow and some wild rocket. The river looked very dirty but the banks had obviously had a lot of love and money thrown at them recently, with a newly refurbished path, flower beds and long lines of quite manicured hedges. The last of these was what really interested me and I was delighted to find that they'd been planted with edible, not just decorative, species, the main 'ingredient' being hazel. Beating the squirrels to the hazelnuts in London is something of an art; too green and the nut is unformed and unpleasant, fully ripened and they will always pip you to the post. There is, however, a stage when the nut shells are still slightly green but have formed proper nuts inside; if harvested at this point you'll have crisp little nuts that taste like tiny avocados. Today, though, I was very lucky; this hedge had just been cut, possibly that morning, and its new haircut had revealed hundreds of ripe nuts which I gathered quickly, stuffing them into my bag with a mixture of guilt and nerves, feeling more like a jewel thief than a forager.

Hazelnut pancakes with a wild flower syrup

More often than not, the hazelnuts that I collect fall into the 'too tasty to make it home' category, but when I have managed to exercise a bit of self-control I've used them to make muffins, biscuits and even a home-made Nutella. To shell the nuts individually takes far too much effort so I prefer to lay them on the kitchen floor and put a big wooden chopping board over the top, standing on it and rocking back and forth until the shells all break. My friend Gemma uses a similar method for acorns, involving an old duvet and a skateboard with its wheels removed. Who says food prep can't be fun?

2 cups shelled hazelnuts, 250g plain flour plus extra (optional), 1 tbsp baking powder, 1 tsp salt, 4 eggs, 350ml milk, 4 tbsp brown sugar, 4 tbsp olive oil

Makes about 20 pancakes

To make the pancake mix, first put the shelled nuts into a blender and whizz them for a few seconds until they produce a coarse flour. Mix a cup of this with the plain flour, baking powder and salt. Then, in a separate bowl, whisk together the eggs, milk, brown sugar and olive oil, before adding to the flour mixture and whisking to form a slightly lumpy batter, adding a little extra plain flour if needed.

Fry the pancakes in a hot oiled pan for about 3 minutes on each side and serve with a fruity syrup. For mine I used April's cherry blossom syrup recipe (page 85), modifying it to include various bright pink seasonal flowers, which included rosebay willowherb, rose petals, poppy flowers and red clover, and adding a vanilla pod for a bit of extra sweetness.

September

A thick and sticky elderberry glaze

Porcini and butternut squash soup

A mixed fruit elixir or cordial or syrup

Blackberry and apple crumble

Very spicy wild plum and crab apple chutney

*'The summer was hardly over but the salad plants, excited
by the warm weather, were all in overdrive and having their
"second flush" earlier than expected . . .'*

ELDER
Sambucus nigra

Five-petalled creamy
white flowers with five
yellow-tipped stamens

Dark purple fruit
hang down from
the trees

Toothed leaflets
in sets of five or
seven

PARTS USED: Flowers, fruit (leaves toxic)

HARVESTING TIP: Don't pick the leaves (they are potentially toxic),
as are the berries if eaten raw . . . so no nibbling!

5th September. Tottenham

I like to call it 'green vision'. Once turned on, it's pretty much impossible to ever turn it off again. Rushing to the Tube is punctuated by flashes of edible plants, just leaving the house turns into an opportunity to look at potential ingredients, and a walk in a local green space will always be brimming with foraging possibilities and culinary ideas. Sometimes it's all a bit too much, even for me! In addition to finding ourselves surrounded by wild food, previously irrelevant spots on the city map can become pivotal and much visited, favourite places to return to with each new season. Today I spent a couple of hours in the grounds of a north London hospital, not because I had anyone to visit but due to the amazing array of fruiting trees planted there. Earlier in the year I'd come here to collect edible tree blossoms: heavenly smelling elderflowers, long 'dangles' of white false acacia flowers, puffy pink bunches of cherry petals and delicate light mauve Judas tree blossoms.

My main reason for today's visit was to look for a true service tree that a friend had mentioned was here, an uncommon and unusual-looking tree, with leaves like rowan and fruit like crab apples. I spotted it immediately, near the entrance, then another and another. In total I found sixteen of them, dotted around the grounds and covered in fruit of varying sizes, although still much too early to pick. I resolved to return in about a month by which time these yellow-red fruits should have turned a chocolate brown and become soft and ripe, their taste and texture like a cross between dates and figs.

As always, there were plenty of other things to interest me, most specifically an enormous amount of perfectly ripe dark purple elderberries. Depending on the season and my location, I have picked these from as early as August and as late as December. Or at least I've picked them that late twice, but from just one tree that grows very close to my house and seems to have a mind of its own. Armed with a big cloth bag, slung 'casually' round my neck, and not wishing to draw too much attention, I set about carefully removing a few bunches from each tree. It always amazes me how many elders there are in the capital; modest and rather dishevelled, they are easy to overlook right up to the point at which they erupt with blossoms in the late spring or early summer, after which they become covered in unripe green berries which I use to make capers. Twenty minutes and probably a hundred good-sized sprays of berries later, my bag was full and my bus was due.

A thick and sticky elderberry glaze

Elderberry wine, elderberry vinegar, elderberry brandy, elderberry jelly, elderberry jam, elderberry cordial, elderberry liqueur . . . Shall I go on? OK . . . elderberry capers, elderberry ice cream, elderberry sorbet, elderberry tincture, elderberry sauce, elderberry tart, elderberry gin, elderberry dye, etc., etc. You get the point, elderberries are very versatile. Not only that, they are nationally abundant, easy to ID and extremely healthy, packed as they are with vitamin C, antioxidants (especially anthocyanins, which give them and numerous other plants their dark purple colour) and other immune 'modulating' flavonoids and alkaloids. The only real safety advice I could give would be, don't eat them raw, they are mildly toxic until they are cooked (or pickled) although reactions vary widely from person to person, some people having no adverse effects and others becoming sick from ingesting just a couple.

700–800g elderberries, 1 litre white wine vinegar, 800g sugar

This simple recipe has been through many hands and seen numerous variations along the way. Although my version is still very sweet and wonderfully tasty, it uses far less sugar than I have often seen recommended. To create a mixture that will cling like thick syrup to the back of a spoon, you need to up the sugar content, literally doubling the amount I use. This will result in something similar to a balsamic glaze, which is fabulous on meat or fish, but I'd suggest trying the less-sugared version first and then having a bit of a play with different amounts later.

Remove the ripe berries from their stalks by running a fork along the stems. Drop them into a big pot of cold water and skim off any that float, then remove all the ripe berries, which will have sunk to the bottom, combining them with the white wine vinegar in a big glass jar. Leave them to sit for about a week, giving the jar a little shake every day or two, then strain the liquid and discard the berries. Put the vinegar, which will now be a rich purple colour, in a saucepan with the sugar and simmer gently for 10 minutes to allow the sugar to totally dissolve before bottling. This will be just thin enough to spray onto food with an atomizer, it makes a delicious salad dressing and goes great with cured meats, roast duck or most freshwater fish. The 'double sugar' version will be too thick to spray but can be used in exactly the same way and is the perfect accompaniment to vanilla ice cream. The flavour of this glaze is truly astonishing. I challenge you not to like it!

PORCINI
Boletus edulis

The cap is light to dark brown, 8–20cm across, and can be slightly slimy when wet

Stems are robust, widening towards the base and pale with a white net pattern

Cream-coloured pores (sponge-like) instead of gills, becoming greeny/yellow with age, producing olivaceous/brown spores

PARTS USED: Entire fruiting body, i.e. the caps and stems

HARVESTING TIP: Check the stems for grubs and also collect bigger, older specimens for drying

12th September. A forest near Tunbridge Wells

As we stood in the car park, putting on our rucksacks and making sure we had all of our climbing kit for the day, my friend Bryan had a confession to make. 'John,' he said, 'I've become a nerd . . . and it's all your fault.' We both knew what he was talking about. I had infected him with my enthusiasm for wild mushrooms, always pointing out the different species we'd see en route to Kent's various climbing areas. Collectively known as Southern Sandstone, these inland cliffs and crags run across most of the county and seem to pop up in the most idyllic woodland locations. Today was no exception, still early in the season (for mushrooms, not for climbing) but numerous varieties were already out. The hike to the crag was only twenty minutes, or at least that would be the journey time for someone not obsessed with what could be found on the forest floor. Surrounded by mature oaks, a few beech trees and plenty of birch and hazel, we set off but only managed a few steps before I stopped. 'Do you smell that?' I asked. 'Stinkhorn!' This phallic and whiffy fungi (*Phallus impudicus*, to give its full title) is easier to find with your nose than your eyes. It's not strictly edible, smelling horrific once it has produced its upright stem and cap, but in the early stages of its growth, the jelly-like egg from which it fruits contains a tiny button mushroom, much prized in Chinese cooking.

We left it untouched, made a couple of obvious jokes and walked on, soon finding something much more interesting, at least in culinary terms. Oh, happy day! A small patch of porcini mushrooms, as the Italians call them, or cep if you're in France. I like the old English name for this delicious edible species, Penny Bun, which gives a very accurate description of the big brown caps that they are famous for, not that anyone in the UK will have seen a real bun that costs a penny for a hundred years. For just a moment I considered leaving them, picking them on the journey back at the end of the day, but my foraging instincts kicked in and I had no choice. There were only a dozen, varying from about 3 to 6 inches; they would just have to come climbing with us, in case someone else stumbled across them while we were busy on the rock. I showed my friend how to pick them, holding the stem at its base and then twisting until the whole mushroom came free. Carabineers, clips, slings and all manner of other climbing paraphernalia got tipped onto the ground; that cloth bag had a more important purpose now. We walked on, two nerds in the woods, arriving at the crag about an hour later than expected.

Porcini and butternut squash soup

There are a million recipes that include this wonderful ingredient, but more often than not I find myself simply frying them with salt and pepper and eating them with as many meals as possible during the season. For porcini in the south of England, this could be just a couple of weeks or as long as three months and occurs anytime from mid-August through to early December. Chefs will always advise adding salt to the frying pan at the last minute, to avoid drying the mushrooms out, but I prefer it added at the start, actually wanting them a little dry and chewy, even verging on crisp, and with their flavour intensified. Gentle cooking will result in a plateful of slugs, lacking in flavour and rather slimy, so don't be afraid to fry them 'hard', although everyone has their own approach so feel free to cook them as much or as little as you like. My favourite way to eat them is just raw, thin-sliced and with a splash of oil and rock salt, a wild fungi carpaccio to make even Carluccio drool. Cep, as the French would say, dry very well and then keep forever. I slice mine 2–3mm thick and either dry them in my dehydrator or spread them out on wire racks and leave them on the stone floor at my mother-in-law's, where the underfloor heating gradually removes any moisture and the house becomes permeated with an amazing mushroom aroma.

1 butternut squash, 2 tbsp olive oil, butter, 1 large onion, 6 garlic cloves, 2 big handfuls of sliced porcini, about 1 litre good chicken stock, dried herbs such as wild marjoram, mugwort, sage or thyme, 1 handful dried porcini or mixed dried mushrooms, salt and pepper, soy sauce and crème fraiche or cream (optional)

Serves 4–6

This hearty soup recipe requires a whole butternut squash, peeled and chopped into 2.5cm cubes, then parboiled for 5 minutes, just to get it started. Keep the seeds for later. In a big saucepan, heat the olive oil with a big knob of butter and then fry the diced onion and crushed garlic (less if preferred). Now add the fresh sliced porcini and fry for a couple of minutes.

Drain the squash and add it to the pan, stirring for a minute before adding the stock, salt, pepper and a pinch or two of any dried herbs you fancy. Then add a handful of dried porcini or mixed dried mushrooms, which will help supercharge the flavour.

Cook slowly for half an hour, adding extra stock if needed. Put everything into a blender or take a hand blender to the pan. There's no right or wrong, so it's up to you how much you blend, how thick the soup is or if you add more stock. At this point I usually add a good slug of soy sauce and, depending on my mood, a couple of tablespoons of crème fraiche or cream. Leave the soup on a very low heat while baking some of the squash seeds (at about 170°C) with a little oil. They take about 10 minutes and taste like popcorn. Serve the soup with the toasted seeds sprinkled over the surface.

ROWAN/ MOUNTAIN ASH

Sorbus aucuparia

PARTS USED: Fruit

Pairs of toothed leaflets

Oval and finely toothed leaves, ranging in colour from green to dark purple

Bright red-orange berries, like tiny apples, with soft white flesh

Fruit can be yellow, red, purple and orange, 2–3cm wide

CHERRY PLUM

Prunus cerasifera

PARTS USED: Flowers, fruit

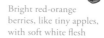

RED SENTINEL CRAB APPLE

Malus x *robusta*

Small, round, bright red fruit

PARTS USED: Fruit

HARVESTING TIP: Wash all these fruits before eating and do not eat rowan berries raw

15th September. Haggerston Park

For four years I worked just around the corner from Haggerston Park without ever paying it a visit. At the time, I was more interested in Shoreditch's warehouse parties and bars than I was in wild food. But today I found myself back in my old neighbourhood, looking for locations for a series of private walks I'd been asked to run near 'the city'. As I headed to the park, the area looked very much the same as it always had, a bit rough around the edges, with the addition of a few more bars and a couple of swanky hotels. The park itself was something of a revelation, playing host to a staggering array of edible wild plants and trees, all packed into a relatively small space, but today more than anything else I was hunting for berries. It's a strange form of human arrogance that we assume bright colours in nature are only there for our benefit, either as a warning or an indication that something is particularly tasty. Some of the most beautiful mushrooms are the most deadly (so are some of the drabbest-looking) and some with the most lurid caps and stems are actually tasty edibles. When it comes to tree fruit, strong reds and purples are often (not always) a good indicator of the plentiful presence of beneficial antioxidants, rather than harmful toxins. I spend the winter months scoffing as many of these genuine superfoods as possible, so today I had it in mind to gather as many varieties as I could and then photograph them to promote my autumn walks.

Bordering a shallow pond was a long thicket of tangled branches, small trees entwined with bushes and shrubs, offering a mix of hawthorn berries (haws), sloes, rowan berries and rose hips. I picked just a couple of dozen of each, popping them into my bag, and then wandered to the other side of the park to examine some free-standing trees and relieve them of a few of their fruits. It was too late for the cherry trees and still too early for the cockspur, but three varieties of crab apple made it into the bag, too. I had easily enough for my photograph, but not wanting to waste what I'd picked I began to think of a new mixed berry recipe.

A mixed fruit elixir or cordial or syrup

However you choose to get your fix of berries, and this could be anything from a hawthorn ketchup to a rose hip vinegar or a blueberry compote, you will be getting masses of fibre, vitamin C and phyto-nutrients. Of the 8,000 or so compounds that have evolved to aid and protect the world's plants, giving them resistance to germs, insects and fungi, many are classified as phyto-nutrients. Although they are enormously beneficial to human health, they are sadly missing from much of our modern food chain. Alas, the presence of these amazing natural medicines has been in decline ever since the advent of Neolithic agriculture 10,000 years ago and generally they have been bred out due to their bitterness. Fortunately they are still abundant and plentiful in wild food.

Last, but by no means least, let's look at the antioxidants – but what exactly are these mysterious substances anyway? Well, I knew that they were chemicals that inhibited the activity of free radicals, but what in turn are they? In the most basic terms (that's how I think), they are atoms or molecules with unpaired electrons that make them very reative and, in this new, free state, can cause various types of cell damage and internal wear and tear, making us susceptible to viruses and numerous other conditions, especially as we get older. I asked a knowledgeable friend to explain how antioxidants combat free radicals. Did they prevent molecules splitting in the first place, or form gangs that went around beating up free radicals, or did they encourage free radicals to reunite with their missing partners and thus stop being free, radical and troublesome? Her answer was a few pages long but basically suggested that they did all three . . . I can't honestly claim to have my head around the science but I wanted to add something by way of research instead of just bandying these terms around without really knowing what they meant.

Mixed fruit (wild and domestic), sugar, 1 cinnamon stick, 2 cloves, 2 or 3 star anise, sugar, honey or xylitol

This is the ideal recipe for any city forager, so take an early autumn wander through your local park or common and come back with just a small handful of any or all of the following berries or fruits: rowan, plum, cherry plum, sloe, hawthorn, medlar, quince, crab apple, pear, rose hip, elderberry, mulberry and blackberry. Supplement what you have with shop-bought plums or soft fruits if you need to. Wash and destalk the smaller ones, chop anything bigger, and put them into a saucepan. With enough water to just cover them, cook for 15–20 minutes with the cinnamon, cloves, star anise and a little sugar, honey or xylitol. Cool and then strain the mix through muslin, squeezing hard to get all the juice out, and then discard the wrung-out fruits. Use as a delicious wild fruit drink, mixed half and half with cold fizzy water, or reheat and add more sweetener to make a cordial – even more and you have a syrup.

BLACKBERRY
Rubus fruticosus

Toothed leaves

Sharp thorns along
the stems

Flowers with five
white petals, often
tinged with pink or
mauve

Berrirs start off pale
green, turn red and then
deep, dark purple

PARTS USED: Young leaf buds, young leaves, fruit

HARVESTING TIP: The sweetest fruit grows on the stem tips,
but handle with care as they are VERY juicy

21st September. Lymington Marina, Hampshire

Unlike many people's relationship with their mother-in-law, I am extremely fond of mine, so staying at her house on the south coast is always a pleasure. She has a huge pond-cum-paddling pool for Oscar and me to play in and, best of all, porcini mushrooms growing around an old oak tree in her back garden. These are one of my fungi early-warning systems and when I hear they are popping up, often as early as mid-August, it's time for me to jump in the car and head to the forest to see what else is happening. Today, when Oscar suggested we go foraging (sweet music to my ears), I knew immediately what he was thinking about, and it wasn't mushrooms. I have never seen a child, or adult, so totally obsessed with blackberries and, fortunately, the coastal path that backs onto the bottom of his grandma's garden is bordered by an almost endless hedge of brambles. When it comes to our 340 species of UK bramble, I'm far from being an expert; in fact were I to be a plant nerd of such epic proportions I would be called a batologist (a botanist who specifically studies this one genus). I can distinguish between a few of the more obvious varieties, but have no real reason to go into greater depth and, more importantly, no spare time for such specifics.

Leaving the house with a little one in tow is never a speedy task but after much faffing and looking for lost wellies we all set off together, the adults taking in the views across the Solent, the Isle of Wight clearly visible on the other side of the water, enjoying the warm September weather that so often these days puts August to shame. Oscar was already focused on the task in hand, a massive grin on his face and a chin dripping with dark juice. I tried to explain that the sweetest berries were the ones on the stem tips and that they'd had the longest time to ripen and produce sugars, but he wasn't listening. Using a rough ratio of three in the mouth to one in the basket, he was surprisingly adept at blackberry picking for a three-year-old, carefully removing the lowest hanging of the ripe fruit and somehow managing to not scratch himself on their thorny armour. We all joined in and our basket began to fill up, although Oscar then abandoned picking any himself, seeming very pleased that everyone else was there to feed his addiction. Telling him I thought he'd had enough for now, I began to carry the basket out of his reach. Tears flowed, small feet were stomped, we ground to a halt and eventually a truce was reached, me carrying both him and the basket, feeding him the odd berry for the rest of the walk. Later I returned for some solo foraging and was able to collect a few hundred without having to trade every third one for a quieter life.

Blackberry and apple crumble

Like elderberries, the list of uses for blackberries is endless. Unlike elderberries, and as everyone knows, blackberries can be eaten raw and it's not easy to beat the pleasure of munching fresh wild berries and fruits straight off the tree or bush they're growing on. The very young unopened leaf buds that appear near me around late February taste like tiny mushrooms, providing you get the timing right; a little too late and they are extremely drying on the mouth or, as my Scottish friends would say, 'It's like licking piss off a thistle'! When the leaves have opened and are bright green, they make one of the best herbal teas and I have also heard of people candying the young stems and then cutting them into thin slices to produce star-shaped sweets. I like to add ripe blackberries to cider vinegar and leave them for a couple of weeks to impart their wonderful flavour and rich colour but my favourite use is in a blackberry and apple crumble, English comfort food at its best.

For the filling: butter, 500g Cox's or Bramley apples, 300g blackberries, 100g brown sugar, powdered cinnamon, 2cm square of ginger root, crème de cassis (also try cherry brandy or whatever sweet liqueur you have)

For the topic: *100g butter, 300g plain flour, 100g brown sugar, 50–70g granola*

Serves 6–8

I think this was originally my mum's recipe but I have made it so many times that it has become somewhat bent out of shape. As with all my cooking, I find it almost impossible to stick to the recipe, but here goes!

Set the oven to 200°C/gas 6 and then grease a big ovenproof dish with butter. Peel, core and chop the apples, preferably a tart variety, and add these to the dish with the blackberries, then cover with the brown sugar. Add a pinch or two of powdered cinnamon, grate the root ginger over the top and drizzle on a little crème de cassis. This I started using because there was a bottle lurking in my cupboard but it could have as easily been something else, cherry brandy, a sweet vinegar or another neglected liqueur.

For the topping, mix the diced butter, plain flour, brown sugar and granola, rubbing it all together until it becomes . . . crumbly. Spoon it evenly all over the fruit and add more drizzles of crème de cassis for good measure. Bake for about 45 minutes and serve with crème fraiche, double cream or, my top choice, vanilla custard.

WILD PLUM
Prunus domestica

Toothed oval leaves

Oval to spherical
bluish-purple fruit

Five-petalled white flowers
with many stamens

PARTS USED: Flowers, fruit

HARVESTING TIP: Unripe fruit will ripen later as long as they are purple when picked,
though they taste best if they are ripened on the tree. Blossoms taste of almond essence

24th September. Tower Hamlets

Although foragers like to think of themselves as adventurous, they are actually creatures of habit and tend to return to the same places repeatedly throughout the year, never straying that far from home for fear that they'll miss something. I once left London for a few days just before my much-loved lime blossoms came out, only to find that on the south coast they were nowhere near ready and by the time I returned to the city they had come and gone. Damn, another whole year to wait for them to come again! Today I visited one of my regular spots, an old cemetery turned nature reserve and a place that I genuinely believe to be the most fertile and diverse square mile in this entire city, if not the whole country. The summer was hardly over but the salad plants, excited by the warm weather, were all in overdrive and having their 'second flush' earlier than expected. At a glance, I could see three varieties of wild mustard, all still in flower (or had they decided to flower again? . . . it's hard to tell these days). A big patch of green in front of me was made up entirely of edible members of the daisy family, sow thistle, wall lettuce, dandelion, nipplewort, ox-eye daisy and scented mayweed (or maybe it was chamomile, it was September after all, not May). There were even a few clumps of late-flowering wild rocket, intensely peppery, as I discovered by munching on a bunch of leaves while I collected some of the other salad ingredients.

Looking to the trees, I noticed that the hawthorn was having an amazing year, huge bunches of red haws hanging from every branch, the sloes (blackthorn) by comparison looked pretty thin on the ground. I wandered, I do a lot of that, you know, and was happy to find that a couple of 'my' favourite wild trees, damsons to be more specific, were covered in fat juicy plums. I think my earliest foraging memory is of plum picking in a friend's garden, using a similar ratio to the one my son applied to his blackberry foraging . . . one for the bag, two for the mouth. I do remember that the end result was a very sore stomach and a stern warning from my mum. Today I would be less greedy and I needed a good bagful for the recipe I had in mind. I'd two-thirds filled my bag before a crab apple tree came into view and I knew that I'd need to pick a few dozen of these, too. As happens to me so often, the recipe had invented, or at least modified, itself to suit what was in season.

Very spicy wild plum and crab apple chutney

1.5kg wild plums, apples and crab apples (that's 1.5kg after removing the unwanted bits, not before), 4 medium shop-bought plums, preferably the red ones, 2 peppers, 500g fresh tomatoes, 8–10 garlic cloves, 4–6 medium-hot green chillies including seeds, 250g red raisins or similar, 250g golden sultanas, 250g black raisins, a big handful of dried white mulberries (optional), 15 cloves, 2 tsp salt, 2 tsp fresh ground pepper, 2 tsp cayenne pepper, 4 tsp star anise (need to be ground up first), 2 tsp dried chilli flakes or similar, 2 tsp ground cinnamon, 2 tsp paprika, ½ tsp smoked paprika, 2 tsp ground coriander, 1.2 litres vinegar (just the cheap stuff), 400–500g brown sugar

This is a big list of ingredients but you can change it around depending on what you have available, miss things out and add others, supplementing the recipe with whatever seasonal fruits you have to hand. Also, you can decide how finely to chop the ingredients depending how smooth or rough you want the final chutney to be. Either way, this is a super-spicy condiment and everyone who tastes it demands the recipe – everyone that is except my mum, whose idea of too spicy is a mild chicken korma. It was previously known as John's Hardcore Winter Chutney and I'd give it away to people at Christmas in jars labelled with a picture of Santa doing something quite obscene. Each time I make this I change the recipe and generally make it spicier than the previous time, but perhaps on your first go, split the batch in two and try making one half as spicy and one half less spicy than my version. I have a tendency to make industrial-sized quantities of this chutney, generally three to four times the amount described here, and I am often asked when I will be making another batch. I always use this request as a chance to enlist the services of the person asking, to help with the endless chopping, and should you find yourself in the same situation, I recommend you do likewise.

Core and stone the plums, apples and crab apples. Chop them into small pieces along with the peppers, tomatoes, garlic and chillies and put all the ingredients except the vinegar and sugar into a big (and I mean big) pan to cook gently for 30–40 minutes, adding about 120ml water if needed. Then add half the vinegar and simmer for a few minutes until the apples are cooked properly, then add the rest and all the sugar. Give everything a good stir, cover the pan and leave it to simmer gently for around 2 hours. Leave to cool and store in sterilized jars. Job done.

October

Pan-fried wild mushroom risotto cakes

Elderberry and clove root cordial

Spicy wild mushroom ketchup

Traditional wild rose vinegar

Sorrel stomp, aka zurkelstoemp

'Mushrooms were popping up everywhere, the fruit trees were heavily laden, brambles and other soft fruits all at their best and, in my neighbourhood, all the springtime salad plants were having a second go, putting up lovely fresh growth and some even flowering, again . . .'

PIED DE MOUTON

Hydnum repandum

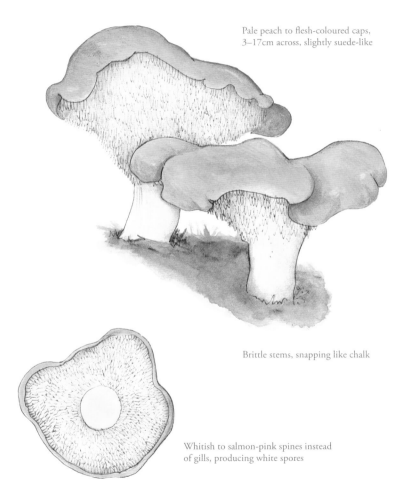

Pale peach to flesh-coloured caps,
3–17cm across, slightly suede-like

Brittle stems, snapping like chalk

Whitish to salmon-pink spines instead
of gills, producing white spores

PARTS USED: Entire fruiting body, i.e. the crop, stems and spines
HARVESTING TIP: Handle these gently to avoid crumbling

1st October. At home in the north of the city

I'd driven back from the woods (a loose title I give to most of Hampshire) the night before, having run two enormously enjoyable mushroom-hunting walks, and for the first time in a good nine months my fridge was half full with delicious and beautiful wild fungi. I have to agree with Italian chef and mushroom obsessive Antonio Carluccio, who evocatively describes mushroom foraging as 'the quiet hunt'. I always find this calming and absorbing multisensory treasure hunt, set in an area of stunning ancient woodland, the perfect antidote to city life. I don't pick any urban mushrooms these days, not that I ever collected many, but having researched the topic at length and studied the ways in which mushroom mycelium is so wonderfully adept at absorbing any and all toxicity that it encounters, if I want to indulge my autumn urges, I get well away from the city. My advice to any novice fungi fancier, go hunting with someone you have 100 per cent faith in and who has a proven track record . . . small mistakes can lead to horrific results and I never, ever, take my ego out with me when I go foraging. If I can't ID what I come across that's absolutely fine, so long as I have no intention of eating it. And in exactly this way, novice foragers can stay safe; if the ultimate destination of a few wild mushrooms is the compost heap not the dinner table, nobody will get poisoned. I know mushrooms are one of the things people are most excited about finding, so I have included recipes for five of my favourite species, all of which are easy to ID, but I can't overstress the need to be cautious and careful.

So, what was in my basket or, more specifically, my fridge? A fine selection of shapes, sizes, colours and smells; mushrooms with some wonderful common names like horn of plenty, pied de mouton, charcoal burner, cauliflower fungus, amethyst deceiver and slippery Jack! A fridge like this, full of autumn fungi, really makes me smile, but it also makes me yearn for the woods, my happy place, they quite literally tug on my heart and beckon me to it. Even if I can't get back there as soon as I'd like, at least I get to enjoy its amazing bounty.

Pan-fried wild mushroom risotto cakes

2–3 shallots, 2–3 garlic cloves, olive oil, butter, fresh herbs, 1kg assorted wild mushrooms, 250g risotto rice, 1 large glass of white wine, 850ml vegetable or chicken stock, salt and pepper

Makes 8 cakes

What's that expression? 'If it ain't broke, don't fix it,' better still, steal it. Sorry, Garry, this is too good not to share.

Peel, finely chop and sweat down the shallots and garlic in olive oil and butter for 2 minutes, add the fresh herbs and the roughly chopped wild mushrooms. Cook for a further 2 minutes, then add the risotto rice, stirring it to soak up the delicious juices and oil. Add the wine and keep stirring until it evaporates, then a ladleful of warmed stock every couple of minutes or so as the risotto gets sticky. Keep stirring and after about 20 minutes stop adding stock (you need the risotto sticky to bind together). Stir in a large dollop of butter and season to taste.

Leave it to cool. Line a flat tray with greaseproof paper, place stainless-steel rings (about 8–10cm wide and 2.5cm or so deep) on the tray and pack tightly with the risotto mixture. Fill as many as you need before carefully removing the ring and setting the cakes in the fridge overnight.

Heat a large frying pan with olive oil and butter and add crushed garlic to flavour the oil before pan-frying your cakes until they are golden brown on both sides.

(Recipe courtesy of Garry Eveleigh, aka The Wild Cook.)

WOOD AVENS

Geum urbanum

Five-petalled
yellow flowers

Red seed heads
with many
protruding
hooked hairs

Lower leaves with gently
serrated edges that become
more pointed higher up
the stem

Lots of long slender roots
that smell of cloves

PARTS USED: Leaves, roots

HARVESTING TIP: Once the root has been dug,
turn over the soil and pat down the earth to allow new seeds to grow

4th October. Inside the M25, but only just

Autumn makes my head spin; the wild world is in hyper-drive, and the extra warmth we get in such a big city adds an additional layer of not so seasonal plant growth into the mix. Mushrooms were popping up everywhere, the fruit trees were heavily laden and, in my neighbourhood, all the springtime salad plants were having a second go, putting up lovely fresh growth and some even flowering, again! Today, realizing that I'd forgotten to make my annual batch of elderberry and clove cordial, and that the city trees had pretty much dropped all their fruit, I headed off in the car, figuring the slightly colder climates out of town would give me the chance to pick from trees a few weeks behind my local ones. I drove just ten miles, almost to my mum's house, before I was rewarded by a line of elder trees, laden with deep purple berries and apparently a good month behind the ones on my doorstep. The difference in temperature may have only been a degree or two but that was all it took. I set to work, armed with my big cloth bag and patented berry hook, a sturdy willow branch that divides to form a large hook at one end and fitted with a long loop of string at the other. I hooked one of the boughs, carefully pulling it down before sticking my foot in the loop of string to keep the stick and, more importantly, the fruit, where I wanted it, and giving me two free hands to pick with. Snapping off each spray of berries and bagging them is the easiest and most effective way to gather large amounts of these tiny fruit.

Normally I'd be happy to use conventional cloves as my other main ingredient, but presented with the low green growth of a common plant called wood avens, it was obvious that I could use it, not least of all due to its other common name, clove root. A member of the Rose family, resembling a strawberry leaf, more rounded and far hairier, it's the roots, not the upper parts of the plant, that have a wonderful nutmeg, cinnamon and clove flavour. So common is this unassuming little plant that, rather than dig them up on the spot (you need the landowner's permission to do so), I just headed home and dug up a few in my own back garden.

Elderberry and clove root cordial

1–2kg elderberries, 500g sugar per 1 litre of liquid, cloves and wild clove roots

I say it's a cordial but it tastes so good that I have never managed to dilute it; instead I drink a neat shot every day throughout the winter. It's not often that pharmaceutical and herbal medicine are in complete agreement but they are when it comes to elderberries. Clinically proven to combat colds, not only a great natural antiviral but also an anti-inflammatory, a diuretic and a decongestant, in other words pretty much everything you need to stay healthy in wintertime. Medicinal properties aside, the joy of knocking back such a tasty treat every day is a fabulous tonic in itself.

Gather a basket of elderberry sprays (at least a kilo, ideally two) and, at home, remove the berries with a fork, dropping them into lots of cold water. Most red or green berries or any shrivelled ones will float, making them easy to skim off, while the ripe ones will sink. Simmer them for 20 minutes in enough water to cover them, plus another few centimetres for good measure. Strain the lot through muslin and wring it out to get as much juice as possible. Discard the fruit before adding about 500g sugar for every litre of liquid, bringing it to the boil and simmering for another few minutes. Bottle in sterilized bottles, adding 15–20 shop-bought cloves per bottle but preferably a mix of these and wild clove root, washed, dried and snapped from the rest of the plant. When digging roots it pays to leave the top of the plant in place to help with identification, only removing it at the last minute. It's the finer lower fronds of this root that contain the flavour, not the tough woody bit that joins the foliage. Give one a nibble to get an idea of the taste – for the experience as much as to judge how much to add. Ready in a couple of weeks but it gets better and better as time passes and the cloves and clove root infuse. Keep some in the fridge and freeze the rest.

As a footnote, when I asked my friend Robin Harford if I could use and adapt this recipe, he responded sagely, 'Of course you can, we're all standing on the shoulders of giants.'

HORN OF PLENTY
Craterellus cornucopioides

The mouth of the tube is wavy, out-turned and up to 8cm across

The whole fungi is deeply tubular with no proper cap

Dark brown to black leathery flesh, drying pale grey

PARTS USED: Entire fruiting body

HARVESTING TIP: Collect in clumps then snap off the bases to remove any grit

6th October. A secret location on the border of Dorset and Hampshire

I'm always excited when I cross that imaginary divide that separates the city from the countryside, and today, driving south to run another two mushroom forays, I had no one to keep me in check. The three-hour journey became punctuated with numerous stoppages, woodland car parks and random detours, finally arriving six hours after departing. Sometimes Ellie suggests we go for a walk, then she'll look me in the eye and explain that this activity involves walking, not just remaining in roughly one spot collecting wild plants or mushrooms. I try to keep moving, I really do, but it's just so hard, especially when my inner child is finally let loose in the seasonal sweetshop of an autumnal woodland. En route, a friend rang, a fellow forager and mushroom obsessive, who's lucky enough to live in an area of gorgeous mature woodland. 'I'm just off to check my secret trompette patch, do you want to join me?' This may not sound that exciting to the uninitiated but for me it would be right up there with offers like 'Would you like to visit my secret diamond mine?' or 'The sheikh would like to invite you to spend some time in his harem.'

Needless to say, I accepted and half an hour later we were both standing outside a relatively famous, very large country pub, me expecting to be blindfolded and driven to this most prized of hidden places. Instead, I followed my friend as we crossed the road, taking literally two steps into the woods before he pointed, not off into the distance but just down at our feet. Trompette de la mort, otherwise known as horn of plenty, one of the most prized gourmet wild foods, with a heady truffle smell and shaped, as you'd expect from their common name, like very dark trumpets. I knelt down to pick the small group of perfectly formed, 4-inch-high horns at my feet and only then, once at ground level, did I really see what he had brought me here for . . . oh my god . . . double take, wipes eyes . . . looks again. Here, in full view of the pub, the road and the pavement, was an endless sea of black, the forest floor gently sloping away for at least a quarter of a mile and everywhere I looked, delicious, extremely sought-after, free food. I'm not a commercial forager and other than for personal use, collecting wild mushrooms in this part of the country is not permitted, certainly not in bulk. Regardless of this I did the maths and realized I was looking at thousands of pounds worth of fungi, at least 200 kilos, and that was what I could see without walking any further. For once, I may have just slightly exceeded the recommended daily picking limit of 1.5kg per person, aware that a week or two later, although easily discoverable by anyone who wanted to pick them, every single mushroom here would have collapsed and rotted back into the soil. What a waste.

Spicy wild mushroom ketchup

I'd already made a trompette omelette, a trompette soup and had trompette on toast with, or for, every meal for the last two days. Oh, and I'd also soaked a couple of handfuls in a good-quality vodka with some red chilli, producing the most wonderful base for a Bloody Mary. Under normal circumstances, I would make this recipe with a less sought-after fungi, but when faced with a glut of these amazing black horns I couldn't help myself.

1kg wild mushrooms, 4 bay leaves, 5 or 6 cloves, 1½ tbsp salt, 1 tbsp dried porcini powder or a few dried porcini, ½ tsp ground ginger, ¼ tsp grated nutmeg, ¼ tsp allspice, 1 star anise, ½ onion, 1 garlic clove, 375ml white wine vinegar, 1 small glass of sweet sherry (optional), black pepper

Mushroom ketchup is a traditional recipe and a great way of using and preserving your favourite fungi. Although the more acceptably produced version is very thin, more similar to a Worcestershire sauce, my creation was much thicker, very spicy and like a dark grey tomato ketchup.

First take the mushrooms, shop-bought if you have no choice, rinse if needed (not usually advised but sometimes necessary with trompette), chop and put them in a large bowl. Add the bay leaves and cloves and mix in the salt before leaving in the fridge for 24 hours.

Remove the cloves and bay leaves, then carefully remove the mushrooms and transfer to a blender, gently pouring the liquid from the bowl over them but making sure there is no grit at the bottom. Blend, then put the mixture in a big saucepan and add about 650ml water and, if you have it, the dried porcini powder – otherwise a few dried porcini mushrooms will do. Also add the ginger, nutmeg, allspice, star anise, the finely chopped onion and garlic, lots of black pepper and the wine vinegar. You can also add a small glass of sweet sherry, but it's not vital.

Bring the whole lot to the boil and simmer gently for an hour, stirring often. Wonderful smells will fill your kitchen until it is time to pass the whole mixture through a sieve to remove any lumps and then bottle into sterilized bottles or jars. I never make the same thing twice so I suggest you play with quantities; you can easily produce a much thinner version with half the amount of mushrooms or more liquid. Keeps for a few months in the fridge.

DOG ROSE
Rosa canina

Five heart-shaped pink petals, becoming white towards the base

Sharp, often reddish thorns

Hard, bright red fruit (hips) with black tips

PARTS USED: Flowers, fruit

HARVESTING TIP: Use scissors and watch out for thorns

10th October. Somewhere in the shadow of Arsenal Football Stadium

It's a tricky time of year for me; the city dweller wants the dry weather to go on forever, while the fungi hunter wants the rain to come and help the mushroom season along. Where I end up foraging is very often in the hands of the gods, so I find it best to just concentrate on the abundance of wild and not so wild fruit that the summer has delivered, and if the weather does turn, then off to the woods I go. Last year was quite literally a wash-out, but this year's alternate periods of hot sun and heavy rain had sent the fruit trees and bushes into overdrive. Like so many of London's best foraging areas, this little gem of a park is tucked away, a magical doorway leads from the street, straight into this wild Narnia. Everything on my picking list was here . . . crab apples, bright orange rowanberries, pears, medlars, hawthorn berries, sloes and blackberries. But best of all, a hedge about 200 metres long, festooned with 2cm scarlet ovals, wild rose hips – dog rose to be specific. I never tire of expounding the health virtues of these amazing fruits. Weight for weight, rose hips contain twenty times the vitamin C of oranges, masses of pectin (commonly used in throat lozenges), high levels of antioxidants, beta-carotene, vitamin B and essential fatty acids, and let's not forget the fact that they taste fantastic.

Rose hips freeze really well and I use them for syrups, sauces and to give sweetness to numerous recipes. I collected about a kilo in under half an hour, a big cotton beach bag round my neck, leaving both hands free to pick as I moved sideways along the hedge like a cross between a crab and a space invader, grinning like an idiot and humming like a bumblebee.

Traditional wild rose vinegar

Rose hips, white wine vinegar or white balsamic vinegar, sugar (optional)

Due to their impressive size, I prefer to pick Japanese rose hips (not a native but thoroughly naturalized) but any variety, wild or otherwise, will do perfectly well and different species will give varying flavours. Part of the joy of this recipe is in the presentation, so if you'd like to end up with bottles filled with rose hips you'll need to use a variety that will make it past the bottle neck and dog rose are one of the most attractive in shape as well as colour.

Another of my recipes that's hardly a recipe at all. Pick bright red hips, ripe but still firm, then top and tail them with a sharp knife before sticking lots of little holes in them with a pin. Be sure not to cause any damage that will let the little hairs from the centre escape. Alternatively, you can freeze and defrost the hips to soften them but I prefer the process of picking and pricking each one. Find an attractive clear glass bottle or jar, depending on the size of your fruit, fill it with hips, then fill the remaining space with white wine vinegar or, if you're feeling lavish, white balsamic. For a sweeter version, heat the vinegar and add a heaped tablespoon or two of sugar to every 100ml of liquid, then leave it to cool before adding it to the hips. About 6–8 weeks later it's ready to use, and in the meantime make sure you leave it sitting around where people can admire your creativity.

COMMON SORREL
Rumex acetosella

PARTS USED: Leaves

Long stems with flowers/seeds
tinged with dark pinkish-red

Shiny leaves with pointed
lobes at the base

HARVESTING TIP: Hold the leaves by the top and shake them to remove any grass

PROCUMBENT
YELLOW SORREL
Oxalis corniculata

PARTS USED: Leaves, flowers

Five-petalled yellow flowers

Trefoil leaves – made of three heart-
shaped leaflets. Green to dark purple

26th October. Richmond Park

Strange, but when out foraging in the city, Richmond Park is exactly the sort of area I avoid, Hampstead Heath, too. It's not that they aren't wonderful places, amazing resources, especially for nature-starved urbanites, and terrific for learning about wild plants, but for me they're just a bit too obvious. When I tell people what I do, how I spend large chunks of my time, these are the places that always get mentioned and although they do hold some wonderful foraging possibilities, I seem to prefer the surprises that less picturesque, less visually appealing spots have to offer. I was always a grubby child, hands in the dirt and staring at the ground, claiming that I was looking for treasure – apparently nothing has changed. Today I visited a relative of mine in Putney; once a towering figure of the music and entertainment industry, these days she prefers to stay home. We spent the morning drinking tea and looking at old photos of her with Lauren Bacall, Frank Sinatra, David Niven, Tom Jones and Shirley Bassey.

I actually don't get over to this part of the city very often; despite its scale, Londoners are basically village dwellers and prefer to stay in their own little areas. So later on, it was a good chance for me to take a walk across Richmond Park and do some very nerdy mushroom spotting (as I have already mentioned, I don't pick any city fungi). There was plenty to see as I walked through the long damp grass: brightly coloured wax cap mushrooms popping up everywhere, lurid shades of red, yellow and green; field blewits with fat white caps and bright purple stems; and even the odd parasol mushroom, huge and visible from a hundred yards away. Another question I often get asked is how often do I go foraging, the honest answer to which is, I'm always foraging, I never stop. Even if I'm not actually picking something, I'm taking in my surroundings, looking at what's in season, what's coming in, what's going out, scoping out new areas and enjoying familiar ones. And so it was that I found myself on autopilot, gathering pocketfuls of delicious common sorrel leaves, crisp and bright green, with an intense lemon meets apple flavour. For safe identification or, more specifically, to distinguish it from a toxic plant called lords and ladies (*Arum maculatum*), make sure the two points that make up the bottom tips of the leaf are exactly that: points, tapering sharply, as if they have been cut with scissors, rather than gently rounded off. It's amazing just how much foliage you can stuff into the pockets of a decent Parka, ironically the same style of coat I'd have been wearing as a treasure-hunting kid.

Sorrel stomp, aka zurkelstoemp

Last year I invented a cocktail with sorrel, pulverizing a bunch of its leaves with a similar amount of apple mint (any mint will do), then adding them to a third of a bottle of good-quality gin. There's only one gin for me, and I'm not going to advertise but it contains twenty-two foraged ingredients and is made on Islay, in Scotland. Also into the gin went some dandelion flower syrup (sugar or honey will suffice), giving it some extra sweetness and a warm orange-yellow colour. We christened the new drink, naming it after my friend's dog Moon, and hence the Moon Dog Martini was born.

Sorrel has multiple uses in the kitchen (tasting as it does, like lemon) and is obviously the perfect ingredient in any seafood dish. I'm not a fan of poached fish but it will certainly bring a zesty lift to some poached salmon, although I prefer mine pan-fried so the skin goes crispy, with the sorrel leaves served on the side. You could also try creamed sorrel with poached eggs or consider adding it to a traditional Turkish lentil soup or mixing into a pea and parmesan risotto. A final thought, common sorrel and the unrelated wood sorrel (often referred to as oxalis) are almost identical in taste and are interchangeable in culinary terms, although the latter looks more like a species of clover. If you find this growing in the city it is more than likely to be one of the various cultivated and feral varieties such as procumbent yellow sorrel.

Potatoes, bacon, sorrel, garlic

I've often considered the possibility that I actually prefer collecting books about wild plants more than collecting the plants themselves, but really one is an extension of the other, and both a bit compulsive. I'm never exactly sure how it happens, but sometimes I end up with three copies of the same book, so last year I asked people to send me their favourite springtime foraged recipes in exchange for a spare copy of Roger Phillips's classic *Wild Food*. The winner was An Vrombaut, who sent me this delicious Belgian dish which literally means sorrel stomp. A simple mix of broken-up pieces of cooked potato (it could be mashed but I plumped for boiled with the skins left on), chopped-up fried bacon and loads of fresh sorrel leaves mixed in, it's a brilliant way to showcase the amazing zesty flavour of this plant. Some fried garlic found its way into mine, too. Wonderful, hearty, peasant food and with sorrel leaves available most of the year, it makes a terrific autumnal breakfast.

November

Hawthorn relish

Hot chocolate made with sweet chestnut milk

A pâté with mixed blewit mushrooms
and sweet chestnuts

Pine needle vinegar with juniper and bay leaves

Candied quince with ginger

*'On reaching a small patch of trees and bushes, mostly
intertwined and surrounded by black-painted Victorian
railings, I was happy to see the fruits I was after, bountifully
dangling and easily accessible . . .'*

HAWTHORN

Crataegus monogyna

The leaves are deeply lobed, particularly the lower lobes

Dark red, oval fruit (haws), around 1cm

Five-petalled white flowers with brown or pink-tipped stamens

PARTS USED: Young leaves, flowers, fruit

HARVESTING TIP: Taste the berries before picking them as the flavour can vary between trees, and look for bigger bunches rather than sparsely growing fruit

2nd November. Highbury Fields

In the years when I was running The Green, a busy gastro pub in central London, I often found myself wandering home late at night, passing Highbury Fields and sometimes doing a couple of laps of it to wind down before bed. I'd never been very good in the mornings anyway, but the stresses of this business would often keep me awake at night. Fortunately my very sympathetic business partner always knew just the right thing to do – send me foraging. 'Chas,' I'd say, 'I absolutely have to go to Devon for three days to pick ransoms so we can have wild garlic mash on the menu,' and he'd always respond, 'Off you go then.' Our menu became peppered with foraged foods; we weren't the first restaurant in London doing this but we were certainly one of them. I don't have the pub these days but I walk through Highbury Fields regularly, sometimes to take my son to the swings, other times on the way to the station and, more often than not, to go foraging, but never due to lack of sleep. Today I headed out with a seasonal favourite already in mind, not only the recipe but the exact location of the tree that would provide me with the ingredients I needed. The sky aimed fat drops of rain specifically down the back of my neck and the muddy ground stuck to my not so sensible canvas shoes, but I was not put off, a man on a mission.

On reaching a small patch of trees and bushes, mostly intertwined and surrounded by black-painted Victorian railings, I was happy to see the fruits I was after, bountifully dangling and easily accessible. Hawthorn is such a superb native fruit, nothing like a juicy plum or a cherry but with a little work they can be made to sing just as sweet a song. I collect very young and pale hawthorn leaves in February and March and use them as a salad ingredient. I think of their flavour as a cross between pea and peanut. Then the blossoms appear, aromatic and with a taste of almond oil common to many members of this group of trees; gently cooked with water and sugar, they make wonderful syrups and cordials. Today was all about the fruit, though, haws to give them their correct name, deep red bunches with twenty to thirty berries in each. With literally hundreds of varieties of hawthorn it's possible to find them in fruit from late August to late December and this tree, just as it had done the year before, peaks in early November. It's easy to grab large handfuls of haws but I prefer to take a few each time in the hope of leaving the stems behind. I stuffed them into my bag until I had nearly two kilos (at a guess) and figuring this was all I needed I headed for home, eager to get busy making a fabulous hawthorn relish. Unsurprisingly, I was unable to make it across the park without also collecting two of my favourite savoury wild herbs, feathery-leaved yarrow (page 233) and some dried-out but strong-smelling mugwort (page 131), both of which would make the perfect flavourings for my recipe.

Hawthorn relish

500g haws, 300ml cider vinegar, finely chopped mugwort and yarrow leaves (optional), 2 star anise, ½ tsp chilli powder, 100g brown sugar

I call this a relish but you could also say it was a chutney, or a smooth pickle, a ketchup, a spicy sauce or even a dip. It seems to change its vocation depending on whether you put it in a bottle or a jar, so you're welcome to fiddle with the recipe and even give it an entirely new name, I'm not precious about these things. If you have any leftover haws, they can be incorporated into some fruit chews with my recipe from January (page 24) or used instead of the cockspur berries in December's jelly (page 244).

First remove the stems from the haws and give them a good wash. Now bring them to the boil with 300ml water and the cider vinegar. I also added a small handful of finely chopped mugwort and yarrow leaves but they are not vital. You could split the batch in two and try some with and some without but if you do this I'd suggest starting with a kilo of haws and doubling the other ingredients to match. In addition to wild herbs, I usually grab whatever comes to hand in the kitchen and have found this recipe really benefits from the addition of a couple of star anise and some chilli powder.

Stir and then simmer everything gently for 45 minutes before removing the star anise. Now the laborious bit, pushing the mushed fruit through a sieve using a big wooden spoon until you have a delicious purée to put back in a clean pan. Never trust a recipe that says this is easy, it takes a bit of time – a food mill makes the job much quicker though. A little at a time, add the brown sugar, gently heating the mixture and stirring until the sugar is properly dissolved. Go easy with it and taste it as you go along, lots of recipes recommend as much as twice this amount of sugar but there is no point smothering the rest of these amazing flavours with sweetness when you can always add more later. The end result is roughly the texture of a thick home-made ketchup, so you can decide what you store it in and what name you use to describe it. Either way, the effort will have been worth it and your only regret will be that you didn't make a bigger batch. Remember to sterilize whichever containers you choose to use and it will keep in the fridge for months, if not years. I spread this on everything, eat it with cheese and biscuits, pour it onto meat like a spicy sauce, dip chips in it and even use it as a pizza topping.

SWEET CHESTNUT
Castanea sativa

Green spiky cases which dry
brown and split to reveal the ripe
chestnuts that are flat on one side

Long, toothed leaves

PARTS USED: Nuts

HARVESTING TIP: Ripe chestnuts will either have fallen to the ground or will fall easily
from the tree if knocked with a stick

12th November. Forty Hall Organic Farm, just in London

Today was brilliant: a private foray for a wonderfully enthusiastic bunch of trainee foragers, novices to the world of wild food but mostly knowledgeable botanists and herbalists, so I needed to be on top of my game. This stunning spot has a rural feel despite its urban location, mixing meadows and rivers with an area of woodland, and giving us numerous wild plants, fruits, nuts and mushrooms to look at and collect. All this and only seven miles from my house. I'm sure I learnt more from them than they did from me but everyone benefitted and our two-hour walk ended up closer to four hours long. It had rained hard yesterday morning, so the ground was still damp, but the air was warm . . . perfect conditions for mushrooms.

   Nestled in long grass we found our first edible species, a ring of ivory-coloured snowy wax caps, a tasty and common grassland fungi, but with a couple of deadly lookalikes, not something for inexperienced foragers to pick. I explained the key ID features to the group, we picked just a few and moved on to look at some other closely related species, their caps much easier to spot with lurid shades of orange, red and green. Under a mature silver birch we found a couple of birch boletus, edible mushrooms that grow in tandem with this species of tree and share a symbiotic relationship with it. The tree supplies the fungi with sugars and in exchange it benefits from a greater ability to absorb nutrients from the soil, its root system getting extended by the mushroom mycelium (the network of white fibres under the ground that produce the mushrooms). Next we spotted a group of edible field mushrooms, again discussing the specifics of identification and adding three or four of them to our basket. Soon a few salad plants joined them: common mallow, young yarrow leaves, dandelion, chickweed, ox-eye daisy and lemon balm.

   It was time to head into the woods and as well as various other edible, inedible and poisonous types of fungi, the thing that interested me most were the unusually plump sweet chestnuts, a common sight in many of our city parks, and fuelled by a sodden spring and a scorching late summer they were almost as big as those we import from Europe. My 'forager's greed' kicked in and I was left with no choice but to suspend the discussion and gather a big bagful, some from the ground and others, ready to drop, were just teased from the tree with a long stick. The whole group joined in and it reminded me of a kids' party where everyone gets a little bag of treats to take home with them at the end of the day.

Hot chocolate made with sweet chestnut milk

What a wonderful crop of 'home-grown' sweet chestnuts we had this year, abundant and much bigger than usual. Come the autumn, most decent greengrocers sell the larger imported varieties but nothing beats cooking and eating something tasty that you have picked with your own hands and, as the saying goes, size isn't important. These nuts are a wintertime favourite in the UK, the basis of a great stuffing or nut roast and the obvious accompaniment to festive Brussels sprouts. For a change, and because I had collected so many, I decided to make a nut milk from them.

25–30 good-sized sweet chestnuts, 3–4 heaped dessert spoons chocolate powder, pinch of red chilli powder, pinch of cayenne pepper

I halved the chestnuts still in their shells, and added them to roughly three times their volume of boiling water, cooking them for 3 minutes. I'd suggest up to twice this time for the bigger shop-bought nuts, but they still need a bit of firmness or they will just crumble when you peel them.

Once cooled, I shelled them, also discarding the thin brown membrane covering the nuts (it can be bitter), and then put them and the cooking water into a blender for a good whizzing. That was it. The resulting slightly thick 'milk' could easily have been strained through muslin or thinned more but I was quite happy with it a tad sludgy, especially for making thick, sweet hot chocolate. I gently heated 300ml of my nut milk with the chocolate powder then added the red chilli and cayenne pepper. These gave the drink a spicy lift and brought out all the flavour.

If you can't get sweet chestnuts then try making other milks – almond, cashew, hazelnut – basically whatever you can find. So simple, so delicious, so get on with it!

Staying with the Christmas theme, they also make a perfect snack, as the song says, 'roasted on an open fire'. Should you decide to try this, be sure to slit the shells of all but one of them with a sharp knife to let the air escape. Include the one that's not been punctured and lay them on the fire in a heavy metal pan or dish. Turn or rattle them regularly to prevent burning and then wait. BANG! The unpunctured shell will literally explode after approximately 25 minutes and signal that the rest are ready to eat. Let them cool a little and then prise them from their shells.

WOOD BLEWIT

Clitocybe nuda

PARTS USED: Entire fruiting body
(stems and caps)

HARVESTING TIP: This species fruits
late in the season with the first frosts

Cap 6–12cm becoming wavy with age

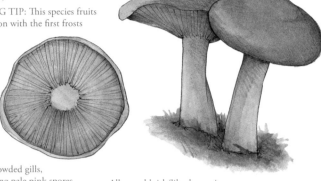

Lilac crowded gills,
producing pale pink spores

All parts bluish/lilac becoming
brownish with age. All parts chunky
and strongly sweet-smelling

Cap 6–12cm, pale then dirty
brown, becoming wavy with age

All parts chunky and
strongly sweet-smelling

Stems
chunky,
pale to
strong violet

Gills crowded and whiteish,
producing pale pink spores

FIELD BLEWIT

Lepista saeva

PARTS USED: Entire fruiting body

HARVESTING TIP: Grows in large rings on grassland

22nd November. Running away to go camping in the woods

Does sleeping in a well-equipped camper van with a pop-up bed in the roof really qualify as camping? I think not, but I'd already decided I needed to escape the city for one last time before my mushroom season came to an end, with the quickest and easiest way being to just jump in the van and get driving. It's the strangest of addictions, mushroom hunting; for roughly nine months of the year I can keep it under control but once the days get shorter and the air damper, there it is again, the monkey on my back, urging me to leave the city behind and take him roaming in the forest. And I love leaving the city at night, the sense of heading off on an adventure and the ease of movement along the normally congested streets. I'm nearly fifty but it makes me feel like a child and with it came the added bonus of camping out rather than making the journey to Hampshire the following morning. Although I'm not a believer in getting up early, even to pick mushrooms, there's certainly something special about spending the night among the trees and waking up in a misty forest.

Joining me was my friend Frazer; tomorrow I would lead a fungi-hunting walk and he would do the cooking, knocking up an epic wild mushroom risotto with some of what we found. He arrived after I did, pulling his battered-looking van up next to my comparatively new and shiny camper. We chatted and he gave my vehicle the once over, seeming impressed with its electric roof, built-in cooker, sink, hidden tables and numerous gadgets. After disappearing into his own van for a few minutes, he returned and casually mentioned, 'It's gonna be a cold one tonight, a shame your posh van's got no heating.' Opening the side door to his own vehicle, he showed me the bed he'd built himself, the wooden cupboards, shelves filled with food and cooking equipment and his dog Tink, asleep in front of the fire . . . *The fire!* This clapped-out-looking van had it all, including a log-burning stove, its chimney poking out of the roof and happily puffing wood smoke into the trees above us. And it really was a cold night. While Frazer and Tink slept like babies, I ended up wearing three pairs of socks and a woolly hat; at least they brought me a hot cup of tea in the morning. After some breakfast we set up the cooking tent and headed to a forest car park to meet our group.

Mushroom hunting this late into the season usually consists of finding four to five 'hero' edible species and a few others to brighten the basket, so after some introductions we set off to see what we could find, me with two or three specific spots already in mind. Along the edge of a grassy woodland path, rutted with tractor tracks, we stumbled on our first and most impressive species, trooping funnel caps, a dozen or so in the group, pale orange-pink, with huge concave caps and some standing nearly a foot high. A great start to the day and soon followed by a few patches of low-growing, pale orange hedgehog mushrooms, another excellent find. Two hours later we'd looked at various edible and poisonous species and picked a dozen egg-yellow chanterelle and a couple of hundred, much darker, winter chanterelle (from a patch of thousands). Our basket looked great but the yellows, oranges and browns needed something different, a splash of bright purple to set them off. This came in the form of a small group of wood blewits, chunky trumpets almost the colour of blueberries, scented like the brick-shaped violet sweets we had as kids, the ones that came in their own cool little dispenser. As we walked I explained the relationship between the mushrooms and the forest, their interdependence and mutually beneficial relationships, the role of fungi and the mycelium that creates them, managing all manner of diverse eco-systems, not just our forests and fields.

Back at camp, Frazer delivered the goods, taking over the session, cooking, dishing out drinks and entertaining the guests, a welcome rest for my throat. Everyone left with a few mushrooms and a greater appreciation of our precious and dwindling woodland, or at least I hope they did. Frazer and I parted company and, as I always do after a woodland walk with a group, I headed back out on my own, maybe not to reclaim the space but certainly to experience it alone, without conversation or a need to please anyone else. I picked a dozen more wood blewits and in a small field that joined the woods half a dozen field blewits, with pale cream caps and electric purple stems. That was all I needed; it was time to head home.

A pâté with mixed blewit mushrooms and sweet chestnuts

1 onion, 300g mushrooms, marjoram, 200g sweet chestnuts, 200g cream cheese, 1 tbsp white wine vinegar, soy sauce (optional), black pepper, salt

As with all my cooking, nothing is totally exact and the quantities and ingredients vary, depending on my mood and their availability. This recipe combines ripe sweet chestnuts and two species of mushroom that pop up at about the same time of year, the wonderful field blewit and its not so close relative the wood blewit, both of which are stunning to look at, sweet-smelling and with a lovely fruity taste, the obvious partners for a nutty mushroom pâté. Although any decent wild mushroom would do the job, these two seem to work particularly well, but be warned. Unless you are 100 per cent sure you have the right species, PLEASE DO NOT PICK THEM (shouty voice). I'd even prefer you bought your 'wild' mushrooms from a shop rather than pick the wrong variety.

Finely chop and gently fry the onion, then add the chopped mushrooms and a few good pinches of marjoram (wild or otherwise), then continue cooking for just a couple of minutes. Now take the sweet chestnuts, halved but with the shells still on (unless they are already cooked and have come out of a packet – boo!), and boil for about 10 minutes before removing the shells and discarding any of the darker inner casing. Whizz the cream cheese and white wine vinegar in a blender; now add the chestnuts and the mushroom/onion mix and some black pepper.

Blend gently until it makes a smooth paste, taste and season with more pepper, salt or soy sauce as required, before putting the mixture into a deep dish and then into the fridge for a few hours to set.

Alternatively, cook the sweet chestnuts for just a couple of minutes and go for a more textured version. You will find that removing lots of them from the shells really hurts your fingers but it's worth it, it really is. Serve with savoury biscuits and a sweet pickle or chutney.

In addition to the general safety advice about mushrooms, I've met a few people across the years who don't get on with these species of mushrooms, finding they get an upset stomach. As with trying any new food for the first time, go easy, try a little rather than eating an entire portion.

SCOTS PINE

Pinus sylvestris

PARTS USED: Leaves
(needles)

HARVESTING TIP:
If you're collecting any
quantity use secateurs

Cones with a raised bump in
the middle of each scale

Long blue-green,
needle-like leaves

The bark is orange-
brown and scaly

Pointed green leaves, with a white
band down the middle of the
inward-facing side

JUNIPER

Juniperus communis

PARTS USED: Leaves (needles), cones ('berries')

HARVESTING TIP: Wear thick gloves as the
needles are sharp. The berries only ripen blue in
their third year

Cones are green when
young, ripening to dark
blue

25th November. Springfield Park

One of the best things about this type of 'work' is the diverse characters that I come across. In just the last couple of years I've been lucky enough to meet and exchange ideas with professional chefs, herbalists, doctors, fellow foragers, survivalists, teachers, nutritionists, local historians, ecologists, botanists, ethno-botanists, mycologists, marine biologists, conservationists and just about every other sort of 'ists' that I can think of. It's often hard to stay on the wild food path and not be seduced by these myriad options and the incredible people involved in them. I've also been able to connect with numerous like-minded individuals and perhaps most enjoyably with other foragers, professional and amateur, at home and abroad. I've learnt so much from this amazing pool of collective and individual knowledge, in person and online, comparing notes and ideas; just five minutes in the company of a friendly Lithuanian couple I bumped into in the woods this time last year gave me three 'new' edible mushrooms to consider (different cultures have very different views on what is and isn't considered edible, especially when it comes to fungi). So today, while carefully removing a few spikes of foliage from a juniper tree, actually more a scraggly bush, I was unsurprised to find myself talking to a total stranger about what I was doing and the uses to which I would put it. He seemed interested, asked me a few questions and then, by way of exchange, proceeded to tell me the social and political history of juniper in this country, most interestingly the role that gin had played in the industrial revolution. In short, the price of alcohol dropped considerably around this time and as a result, the working classes were kept in two subdued states, drunk or hung-over, for over sixty years. Cheap beer and gin played a large part in keeping people in line and, if not tolerating, then less able to object to the appalling living and working conditions that were forced upon them.

I showed my new friend how to ID juniper, a task best performed with the nose (a crushed sprig really does smell just like gin), as well as looking at the shape, colour and arrangement of the needles. We parted company and I walked across the park to hunt for a few wild salads and to look at more conifers. Juniper is an uncommon sight in London and scarce in much of the UK excluding northern Scotland. When I'm lucky enough to find any there are never any berries (actually they're not true berries but the female cones), they take two to three years to ripen and either they don't fruit here or the squirrels get there first. This isn't a problem, as I find the needles of these and numerous other pines, firs and spruces to be excellent as flavourings and available all year round, although probably at their best in the spring. Before heading home, I visited a few other trees, a Scots pine, a stone pine and a spruce, relieving each one of a few twigs or bunches of needles. Resinous smells wafted from my bag and ideas for sauces, syrups and vinegars filled my head.

Pine needle vinegar with juniper and bay leaves

It's a good idea to learn how to identify a yew tree (or bush, or hedge) if you intend cooking with any of the other conifers. Almost all parts of yew are extremely poisonous (excluding the outer flesh of the berry) and even so much as a nibble could be dangerous. Fortunately, this is a very easy species to ID, with its dark green needles arranged in a distinct fishbone pattern, one row on each side of the stem (this isn't quite botanically accurate but visually it's correct).

So, moving on, last year I made a delicious syrup by cooking the needles of Douglas fir in a little water, then blending the water with sugar and honey until it thickened. While it lasted, I poured it on my cereal every day, although it would just as easily have made a great cocktail ingredient and mixes superbly with gin. I've also seen it used to flavour custards, sorbets and yogurts, and there are numerous pine-based booze recipes, perhaps most notably the Greek wine, retsina. Trying to keep my booze intake to a minimum, especially ahead of the inevitable festive excesses, I plumped for making a flavoured vinegar and found that the end result not only gave a

wonderful lift to salads and dressings, it made the perfect substitute for rice wine when it came to making sushi rice.

400ml apple cider vinegar, 2 handfuls of mixed pine or fir needles, 4 juniper twigs, a handful of dried juniper berries, 4 bay leaves, 2 heaped tbsp brown sugar

Add the apple cider vinegar to 100ml water, heating them both gently in a saucepan. Next add the mixed pine and fir needles as well as the juniper twigs. Also into the pan went a handful of dried juniper berries (I bought these) and the bay leaves. Let everything simmer gently for about 15 minutes before adding the brown sugar, allowing it to dissolve before pouring the liquid into a large sterilized glass bottle. I then added the needles, twigs and berries to the bottle, partly for effect and also to allow them to carry on infusing. The taste reminds me of being outdoors, and the bottle makes a great table decoration and conversation topic.

Every day for the next week, I used the leftover needles to make a herbal tea, steeping them in boiling water for 10–15 minutes, high in vitamin C and extremely refreshing. Pine needles can impart a wonderful flavour to meat and fish, try roasting lamb or beef with a sprig of Scots pine instead of rosemary. I've also seen mussels smoked over spruce tips and venison roasted in a wonderfully aromatic pine needle and vegetable stock.

QUINCE
Cydonia oblonga

Five-petalled white/ pink flowers with many stamens

Leaves with untoothed edges and pointed tips

The fruit is bright yellow, shaped like a swollen pear

PARTS USED: Fruit

HARVESTING TIP: The fruit is completely yellow when ripe and comes off the tree easily

27th November. A street close to Highgate Woods

In the present day and in an urban setting, going foraging can just as easily involve the use of a little modern technology as it does wandering happily with a basket, hunting for seasonal delights. I have various favourite bits of high-tech equipment, including my van, complete with a stove and all manner of baskets, bags, boxes and tools. Back in January I sang the praises of my freezer, which allows me to vastly extend the usable seasons of numerous wild plants and preserve them without having to add masses of sugar. My dehydrator, running pretty much full time, has helped me create a huge and diverse native spice rack to use in my cooking. Online satellite maps are wonderful tools for scoping out potential foraging sites, especially good spots for mushroom hunting. And lastly, I am slightly ashamed to admit, the smartphone. Not only does it mean I always have a camera on me, it allows me access to maps, GPRS, weather reports and today, best of all, to receive a foraging tip-off from a friend. Foragers are a generous bunch, aware as we are that the foods we collect are free, we like nothing better than sharing our bounty, so this morning's text from my friend Gemma was nothing out of the ordinary. It simply read 'Want to pick some quince?' This meant that the tree in her neighbour's garden was now in full fruit and I should head over, which I did later in the day.

Quince trees are rather small and squat, producing large yellow fruit shaped like a cross between an apple and a pear, both of which they are related to. The tree that I'd come to see was hardly more than a big bush and weighed down with more fruit on it than I'd ever seen on one before, probably 150 fat yellow 'pomes', each weighing about a third of a kilo. We knocked on the door and the neighbour, who seemed to be expecting us, told us to help ourselves, eyeing his tree with a 'rather you than me' sort of expression. We needed no further encouragement and as we picked, warmed by a low orange sun, we discussed the many uses to which we could put this wonderful free food. Unlike apples and pears, quince do not taste good straight from the tree; they're too tough and far too acidic, but once cooked, candied, poached or pickled, they really are a world-class fruit. I was very happy with my heavy bagful and although the walk home was a couple of miles and the temperature had taken a sudden drop, I spent the time thinking of all the recipes I could remember and inventing a couple of new ones, too.

Candied quince with ginger

Apparently the first quince tree in England was planted at the Tower of London in 1275, ordered from Europe by Edward I. Exactly when a tree or plant becomes 'native' is a debatable topic but, regardless of its origins, I think of these as one of our greatest old English fruits. It's worth mentioning that there are also four species of ornamental bush, collectively known as Chaenomeles and commonly referred to as Japanese, Chinese, flowering and dwarf quince. Although they produce smaller fruit, all can be used in exactly the same way and are a far more common sight in the city than the trees are. The most frequent use for quince is in making jellies or jams, most notably membrillo, a thick preserve made from the pulped fruit and originating from Italy, Spain and Portugal. Numerous regional variations exist all over Europe and South America; generically referred to as quince cheese, they are usually served as an accompaniment to hard cheeses or cooked meats. The recipe below was generously given to me by Katherine Taylor, quince lover and author of the excellent food blog anediblelandscape.wordpress.com.

1kg quince, 500g brown sugar, about 1 tbsp ground ginger

Wash, peel and core the quince before cutting them into bite-sized pieces. Place them in a large bowl, sprinkle with the brown sugar, cover and leave to marinate for 48 hours, after which lots of liquid will have appeared. Strain this into a saucepan using a sieve, then put the quince pieces back in the bowl and set aside. Bring the juice in the pan to the boil and simmer for 4 minutes before pouring it back over the pieces in the bowl. Cover and leave to marinate for 24 hours. Repeat this process twice over the next two days and finally bring the quince pieces and the juice to the boil together and simmer for 5–10 minutes. Remove from the heat, stir in up to 1 tablespoon of ground ginger and pot in sterilized jars. Stored in a cool, dark place the candied quince will keep for many months. Serve as an accompaniment to meat and cheese (in northern Italy they also use it as a tortellini filling) or else with toast and croissants, or as a fragrant addition to apple pies and other bakes.

December

Quick pickled winter chanterelle with rice wine,
chilli and garlic

Blackthorn and elder pacharan with vanilla
and coffee beans

Yarrow, lavender and rosemary oxymel

Wild sushi rolls with bellflowers, bittercress and salad burnet

Cockspur jelly

*'Nature is just so unpredictable, wonderful and confusing; very
often I concede that my purpose is not to reason why it does
what it does, but to just be in the right place at the right time
and gratefully receive its gifts . . .'*

WINTER CHANTERELLE
Craterellus tubaeformis

Darkish brown caps, 2–5cm, convex
with a depressed centre and a wavy
edge

Light yellow to grey ridges
running down the stem,
producing yellowish spores

Stems hollow, grey
to dirty yellow

PARTS USED: Entire fruiting body, i.e the caps and stems

HARVESTING TIP: Collect in clumps then snap off the bases – don't bother with a knife

1st December. At a friend's in Walthamstow, post fungi-hunting in Essex

'When are you going to take me mushroom hunting then?' If I had a penny for every time I'd been asked that question I'd have, well, about £1.50, I think. The trouble is, I am always ready to head out but when that rainy Sunday morning comes round, most folk are not as keen as they were in the pub the night before. Today was the exception, the sun was out and at 8 a.m. my over-enthusiastic friend was banging on the door and insisting I made good on my promise. The horrific task of driving in London becomes an absolute joy when no one else is on the road and just over an hour later we were standing in a woodland car park, most of the way to Cambridge, drinking tea and putting on our boots. I love the woods when they are like this, crisp underfoot, chilly on the breath but warm enough to not need a coat, and with that heady, late-autumn smell on the air. A forest clearing, a shabby lawn bordered by majestic oak trees, provided the ideal spot to hunt for the last of the season's porcini mushrooms, but despite our search, none were to be found, most had fruited earlier in the year, and the temperature was now too cold for them to 'come again'. As they say, that's just how it goes.

We walked on, finding a patch of hedgehog mushrooms, pale orange, almost peach-coloured, nestled in the leaf litter. They grew in a wide banana-shaped arc on the forest floor, in the shadow of a huge beech, a 'mother tree', probably 150 years old and obviously responsible for the numerous younger trees that surrounded it. They gave a good weight to our otherwise empty basket but the real pleasure came less from what we picked, more from the hunt and the opportunity to walk in the woods together. Half an hour later, on the border of the beech woods and a pine plantation, we realized that we were surrounded by winter chanterelle, so many mushrooms that they seemed to have crept up on us, not the other way round. Growing often in patches of many thousands, this wonderful little fungi has a cap that looks very much like the fallen foliage in which it flourishes, 'hiding in plain sight' summing up its appearance perfectly. Once flipped over, it reveals a long yellow stem, which gives it another of its common names, the yellow leg. Faced with such a prolific and tasty mushroom as this, no conversation was needed, just quiet, methodical picking, a perfect mix of calm and excitement until the basket was full and a spot of rain told us it was time to head home.

Quick pickled winter chanterelle with rice wine, chilli and garlic

Some winters I pick this amazing frost-resistant fungi when there is snow on the ground and even though I'd waited almost a year for them to come out so I could make this pickle, I can see no reason why it wouldn't work equally well with all sorts of other mushrooms, although it won't look quite as lovely. This is a great recipe, ready the day after you make it and perfect to bring a bit of zing to any winter plateful. It took six texts, four tweets, five emails and three requests in person before Rob, head chef at Clerkenwell's Modern Pantry, generously gave up this most prized of culinary secrets.

40g peeled ginger julienne (thin-sliced, in other words), 5 finely sliced garlic cloves, 2 medium deseeded and finely sliced red chillies, 40g fresh green peppercorns (substitute capers if needed), 150ml extra virgin olive oil, 1kg winter chanterelle or similar, 100ml rice wine vinegar, 50ml soy sauce

Sauté the ginger, garlic, chilli and peppercorns in the oil until fragrant and soft. Add the mushrooms and fry for 2 minutes. Add the vinegar, soy and 50ml water and cook for another minute before removing from the heat. Leave for 24 hours to pickle/marinate before serving. This is a zesty Japanese-style 'light' pickle so I imagine it won't last for months like a traditional preserve.

As a footnote, I'd always suggest dry-frying (without any oil) the winter chanterelle for a minute beforehand, which will allow them to release some water, so when you do come to cook them they will fry rather than just poaching in their own juices. This liquid can be reserved and used to make a mushroom gravy. On their own winter chanterelle are delicious fried with brown (caramelized) butter and although they become tiny, they dry very well so can be used as an addition to soups and stews throughout the year.

BLACKTHORN
Prunus spinosa

Dark purple berries with a light
blue bloom that rubs off

Small (2–4cm) oval
leaves with serrated edges

Five-petalled white flowers
with many stamens

Blackish-purple
bark, often with
sharp thorns

PARTS USED: Flowers, fruit

HARVESTING TIP: Be sure to avoid the spines; splinters from them can cause serious infection

3rd December. Hampstead Heath

Accentuated by the utter absence of anyone else, which is unusual for this huge patch of London greenery, and the presence of a low-hanging mist floating just above the damp grassland, the oddest of sights greeted me today as I took a walk on 'the heath'. It appeared to be more the result of witchcraft than any natural phenomenon. A hedge of blackthorn bushes, hundreds of metres long, naked and skeletal as one would expect right now, except that every 15 metres or so was a big patch of extremely late fruit, vastly exceeding its 'fall-by' date. Sloe is the more common name for blackthorn, and generally used when describing these small purple plums and the festive flavoured gin for which they are famous. The traditional time to harvest is much earlier in the year, when the first frost arrives, this deadline having the dual purpose of cracking the skins to help release flavour and also allowing the fruits as long as possible on the branch to make plenty of sugar. As anyone who has tasted raw sloes will tell you, even when fully ripened they are extremely drying, being very high in tart-tasting tannins. Finding myself at a loss as to the cause of this weird, wild alchemy, I collected what I could, already considering what this fortuitously late bounty should be used for. Sloe gin? No, too predictable. Sloe jam? No, it would just sit on the shelf with all the other random experimental preserves. Something with herbs and alcohol? Yes, that's always a good option; some further research would be needed. I was surprised to find these sloes to be in excellent condition, fat and firm and apparently unconcerned that every other fruit had fallen to the ground a good month earlier. Nature is just so unpredictable, wonderful and confusing; very often I concede that my purpose is not to reason why it does what it does, but to just be in the right place at the right time and gratefully receive its gifts.

Blackthorn and elder pacharan with vanilla and coffee beans

1 litre ouzo, raki or Pernod, 1 litre vodka, 300g ripe sloes, 300g elderberries, 6–8 tbsp sugar, 2 cinnamon sticks, 24 coffee beans, 2 vanilla pods

I could have described this drink as a sloe pacharan, but I think blackthorn sounds more exotic. The recipe comes from the Basque region of Spain and is traditionally made with just sloes and any aniseed liqueur; ouzo, raki or Pernod will all do fine.

I used a litre of Turkish raki mixed with a litre of vodka (I'm such a cheapskate). To this I added the ripe sloes and, finding myself with not enough fruit, supplemented them with the same amount of elderberries, picked and frozen earlier in the year. In a big glass jar, I left everything to infuse for a couple of weeks, allowing the alcohol to take on the wonderful colours and flavours of the fruit. At this stage I added the sugar, the cinnamon and two dozen coffee beans. An authentic pacharan would also include orange peel and chamomile flowers, but I opted for including a couple of vanilla pods, figuring the anise, vanilla, coffee combo would work well. Then the waiting begins. This needs to be left somewhere dark for at least a month, given a little shake every few days and then strained through muslin and bottled.

It will also work very well with just elderberries and although the flavour is delicious after only a month or two, a year later it will have adopted all manner of unusual herby notes and taste more like something made by a sixteenth-century monk than a modern-day forager. I have tried various other recipes with sloes – jams and jellies and even an unsuccessful attempt to mimic Japanese sour plums – but this is far and away the best I have come across.

YARROW
Achillea millefolium

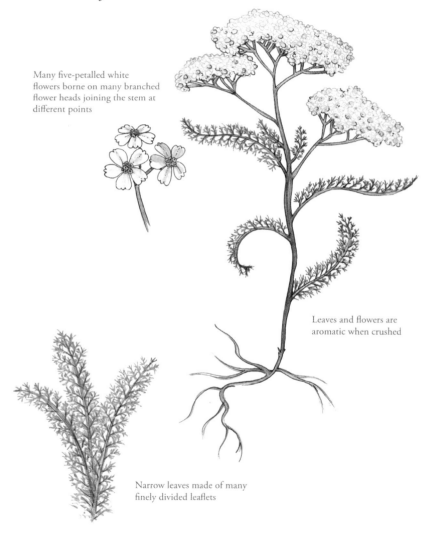

Many five-petalled white flowers borne on many branched flower heads joining the stem at different points

Leaves and flowers are aromatic when crushed

Narrow leaves made of many finely divided leaflets

PARTS USED: Leaves, flowers

HARVESTING TIP: Look for the new foliage on disturbed earth and grassland. The leaves and flowers become more bitter as the year progresses

8th December. Brockwell Park

Today I found myself saying, 'I can't believe I've never been here before.'
This place read like a tick-list of all my favourite winter plants, or at
least those that I find in the city: Michaelmas daisy, ox-eye daisy, yarrow,
lucerne, mugwort, sow thistle, winter cress, feverfew, chickweed, self-heal,
cat mint, nettle, vetch, sorrel, sweet violet, crow garlic, hedge mustard,
hoary mustard, lavender, rosemary and dozens of others. Finally getting
round to visiting an old friend who lives 'south of the river', I found
myself in Brockwell Park, exploring its wilder corners, excited by its
diversity and considering the concept of 'shifting base-line syndrome', an
idea more commonly applied to ecology and natural evolution than to the
social and physical changes of a city. Brixton has moved on enormously
in the last few years, the dreaded and sanitizing effect of what is often
referred to as 'gentrification' has done its worst, or its best depending on
your view; the edginess and the excitement has all gone and the coffee
shops have arrived. Unlike much of London, our parks are something of
a time warp; the signage and the food offerings may have been updated
but not much else has changed. They are still the places we go to clear our
heads or get some perspective, within but removed from the frenzy that
surrounds them. For me, the park is a place where I can look at the bigger
picture, with just enough distance to get a wider view.

Today the city looked like a huge body of water, shifting and flowing,
constantly moving and always changing, and the park, obviously, was
an island, offering a sense of stability and constancy, the purpose for
which it was created and the role it still plays. Dragging myself away
from my musings, I realized that my friend was waiting for me at his
house and I was late. 'Under the weather' was how he'd described himself
and I'd promised not only to keep him company but to bring him some
fortifying wild plants. A nearby flower bed waved at me, literally (it was
a windy day), so I grabbed a small bunch of three wonderfully aromatic
woody plants and headed off to my friend's house to create a warming
winter tonic.

Yarrow, lavender and rosemary oxymel

350ml cider vinegar, 225ml thin honey, a handful of yarrow stems and leaves, a handful of lavender leaves and flowers, a handful of rosemary leaves and stems

Vinegars have a long history of use as medicinal cordials, as well as for flavouring and preserving food, and vinegar drinks are having something of a renaissance at the moment, with posh cocktail bars favouring the sweet varieties known as shrubs, infused with fruits, berries or syrups. I love the ease of making vinegar-based drinks and home remedies and they are ideal for all manner of experimentation. Oxymel comes from the Latin *oxymeli*, meaning acid and honey, and traditionally this blend would have been used as a way to administer herbs that were too bitter or unpleasant to take on their own. Numerous recipes exist, many dating back thousands of years, with proportions and ingredients varying enormously, as do the herbs that can be included. This recipe, concocted for my poorly friend, uses only safe, edible plants, and although they have their own medicinal properties I was in no way pretending that I was a qualified herbalist, more that I wanted to give him a soothing winter tonic to help him feel a little better, much the same way as we use a 'hot toddy'.

The reason for the proportions of cider vinegar and honey that I used was nothing more precise than that the vinegar came in a 350ml bottle and the honey in a 225ml jar, so feel free to play around and make your own version more or less sweet, thicker or more runny. I gently heated both together, just long enough for the honey to melt, then stirred in a chopped-up handful of yarrow stems and leaves, the lavender and rosemary. When it had cooled, I used a couple of tablespoons of the mix to make my friend a delicious tea and I put everything else into a sterilized jar, telling him to leave it there for a couple of weeks before straining out the plant matter. This, or any similar blend, can be taken daily as a tonic, used like a cough mixture when needed or drunk as the base of a herbal tea.

For an alternative use for these three herbs, consider using them ground in savoury muffins or wrapping them round any fatty meat that you are roasting; they all have their own slight bitterness, so will let your digestive system know it's time to spring into action.

WALL BELLFLOWER

Campanula portenschlagiana

Purple flowers with five petals that join to form a bell-shaped base

Heart- or kidney-shaped toothed leaves

PARTS USED: Flowers and leaves

HARVESTING TIP: Select plants that grow on higher rather than lower walls, out of the dog-wee zone

20th December. Alexandra Palace

If foraging teaches us anything, it's to enjoy and celebrate what is available, not to hanker after what is not. If only I/we could carry this simple lesson out into every aspect of our existence, especially city life, where everything is demanded and supplied immediately and where choice is infinite and often unappreciated. In a rather less than Zen mindset, I left my house today in a horrid mood, having slightly taken out my computer-related frustrations on everyone I had had any contact with – to my shame, the delivery man who asked me to sign for a neighbour's package getting the worst of it. After an hour or so of despatching various pre-Christmas chores, I headed to the enormous green hillside a couple of miles from my house, partly to forage, partly just for the view, but mostly because I knew that the walk to its summit would tire me out and thus render me less grumpy. Ally Pally, as it's universally known, opened in 1873 as a public venue and was dubbed 'The People's Palace'. In 1936 it was the site of the BBC's first-ever television broadcast and it still plays host to regular exhibitions and concerts, but although it's relatively close to my house I seldom visit it except for the annual firework display. The palace grounds mostly consist of a huge south-facing hill with amazing views across the whole city and are made up of some wonderful, minimally managed, grasslands, meadow and woods; a real treasure for anyone who views the city's open spaces as I do. Today, this close to Christmas, it was very cold and bitterly windy on the exposed hillside and it quite literally blew my bad mood away, leaving me clear headed and able to appreciate my surroundings.

I gathered the ingredients of a winter salad, a mixture of my favourite seasonal greens. First in the bag went some salad burnet, an unassuming little leaf that tastes like a wonderful cross between cucumber and melon. Hot on its heels, the peppery delights of hairy bittercress, growing in big tufts in the middle of a flower bed, one of the few more managed spots here. Next I collected some white dead nettle, with both its leaves and flowers on show, followed by the greeny purple leaves of some young garlic mustard and a small but succulent patch of chickweed. A few other ingredients later and I was heading home, en route relieving a mahonia bush of a few of its bright yellow flowers, and was almost at my front door when I bumped into one of my favourite and most used city salads, wall bellflower. This plant absolutely thrives in urban locations, often growing in a conveniently elevated position, as its name suggests, out of a wall. With deliciously lush greenery and sweet purple flowers, I am able to pick this almost all year round. As I walked in the door, I picked up a sushi menu that had been pushed through the letterbox. Eureka! Who wants a salad when you can have sushi, or better still, wild sushi?

Wild sushi rolls with bellflowers, bittercress and salad burnet

They say that Scotland is a country of great innovations: the telephone, the steam engine, the deep-fried Mars bar, to name but a few. So it comes as no surprise that my friend Mark Williams, Scotland's foremost authority on wild food, should come up with an idea bordering on genius! I'm often asked about the best way to cook or consume the foods we forage for and I always come back to the same thing – keep it simple. If it already has a great taste then why mess about with it or mask it under layers of other flavour? This is why Mark's idea of using wild ingredients to make sushi provides such a superb platform for experiencing the delights of our wild larder, without the confusion or conflict of too many other ingredients. Below is a simple recipe for preparing sushi rice but I would not presume to tackle such a huge topic in just a few words and I'd suggest a good sushi cookbook would be more informative. With endless possibilities, it really is up to the individual to decide what to make and how best to approach it, but for my version I

SALAD BURNET

Sanguisorba minor

PARTS USED: Leaves

HARVESTING TIP: The leaves are
tastier and more succulent before
flowering

Long leaves made of pairs
of many-toothed leaflets

Produces lots of flowering stems with
seed pods running down them and tiny
white four-petalled flowers at the tips

Grows in bushy tufts

BITTERCRESS

Cardamine hirsuta

PARTS USED: Leaves
(including the stems), flowers

HARVESTING TIP: Cut at
the base of the rosette to keep
the leaves together

Rosettes of twenty or more leaves
with tiny white hairs, especially on
the ends of the leaflets

created a selection of maki, small rice rolls, wrapped in sheets of nori seaweed, with a selection of my wild salads in the centre, seasoned with soy and Japanese horseradish, aka wasabi. For a native wasabi, consider using one of the more spicy relatives of cress or mustard, the best being a small coastal plant called scurvy grass.

3 cups (600g) shari (sushi rice), 120ml rice vinegar, 4–5 tbsp sugar, 4–5 tsp salt, nori seaweed sheets, assorted wild leaves and flowers

For the rice, cook the thoroughly washed shari in the same volume of water plus about 10–15 per cent extra. Bring it rapidly to the boil, stir it occasionally and then cover and cook it on a low heat for about 8 minutes. With a wooden spoon, carefully remove the rice, avoiding any that's burnt or overcooked from the bottom of the pan and transfer it to a wide wooden or plastic dish to cool. Now mix the rice vinegar, sugar and salt, gently heating them before pouring onto the rice, carefully mixing it all together and then letting the rice cool again, but not in the fridge. That's it – now grab your rolling mat, your nori and your wild salads and get rolling, perhaps having watched an online tutorial first.

COCKSPUR

Crataegus persimilis 'Prunifolia'

Small, round, red fruit, with five-pointed remains of the flowers on the tips

Long thorns

Dark green, toothed leaves

PARTS USED: Fruit

HARVESTING TIP: Avoid the huge spines on this super armoured tree . . . it's not looking for a fight but it's ready for one

26th December (Boxing Day). Roaming the streets of London

City life is a paradox, a choice (for most of us) to spend all our time in ridiculously close proximity to vast numbers of our fellow men and women, while at the same time constantly yearning to have more space, a little solitude and a greater sense of individuality. Today, however, London was empty, the streets were deserted, the roads almost unused and the usual level of background noise reduced to nothing more than the odd car and a bit of birdsong. I got the impression that despite the six million people resident in this massive city for the majority of the year, no one was actually a true Londoner anymore. They had all fled, back to their families in the suburbs, the countryside or abroad, as I would usually have done, too, but not this year. What a joy it was to walk down the road without the normal distractions, quietly appreciating the myriad street trees, usually passed in too much of a hurry for most people to even notice. My walk went like this: a pear tree, a cherry plum, a rowan, another cherry plum, a crab apple, a mystery tree, another pear, two hawthorns, a Turkish hazel, an avenue of common limes, a Judas tree, two black locust trees, a sweet chestnut, more hawthorn, another rowan. Then, turning a corner, a cockspur tree, which I had been unconsciously looking for and, unlike everything else I'd noticed – all of which would produce edible fruit, nuts or leaves next year – this was absolutely covered in seasonal decoration, dark red clumps of berries, to be precise.

Cockspur, sometimes called a cockspur thorn, is a non-native relative of our own hawthorn tree, similar in some respects but with oval leaves like those of a plum tree and protected all over by huge aggressive-looking spines. These thorns are an ancient hangover from a time when this tree would have needed to defend itself from large grazing animals, a feature still found on some of our native trees and bushes, most noticeably on sea buckthorn. Unlike almost every other edible tree in the capital, cockspur fruits very late and I have sometimes harvested the berries right at the end of January. Today I picked about a kilo, a task that took just a couple of minutes, each bunch containing thirty or forty individual berries. I wandered home to do some cooking, looking around as I walked . . . pear tree, crab apple, hawthorn, rowan, another pear, and on and on. My walk was ending, the year was, too, but foraging is a cyclical activity, the end of one season only heralds the beginning of another and they overlap so much that there is no time to think about endings, only new beginnings, renewed opportunities and the joy of whatever wild delights are coming next.

Cockspur jelly

1kg cockspur or hawthorn berries, juice of 2 lemons, brown or white sugar (1kg per litre of liquid)

I'm a huge fan of preserves but I generally enjoy eating them more than making them; the endless chopping, the use of masses of sugar and careful temperature controls are just not things that push my buttons. As a result, I'm always looking to create or simplify recipes as much as I can and this is the reason I prefer making jellies to jams, straining what I produce rather than carefully removing any unwanted parts; it's just less work. Cockspur, like hawthorn, produces a delicious, quite stiff jelly, a little similar to a quince 'cheese', probably due to the high levels of pectin found in all of these.

Wash and remove the stalks from the cockspur or hawthorn berries, then, in a big pan, bring them to the boil with 500ml water and simmer gently for 45–60 minutes. Allow the mixture to cool and then strain it through muslin, wringing it out vigorously to get the maximum amount of liquid, then add the lemon juice and measure the volume before putting it into a clean pan. Add sugar at a 1:1 ratio, i.e. for every litre of liquid add a kilo of sugar, and bring to the boil, stirring continuously and keeping it at a rolling boil for 10 minutes until it reaches its 'setting point'. Now decant the hot liquid into sterilized jars, being careful to leave any froth behind.

A guide to
the basics
of urban
foraging

A year of urban edible plants

Month	Scientific name	Common name	Scientific name of family	Common name of family
January	*Taraxacum officinale*	Dandelion	Asteraceae	Daisy
January	*Anthriscus sylvestris*	Cow parsley	Apiaceae	Carrot
January	*Barbarea vulgaris*	Winter cress	Brassicaceae	Cabbage
January	*Malus* 'John Downie'	Crab apple	Rosaceae	Rose
January	*Elaeagnus rhamnoides*	Sea buckthorn	Elaeagnaceae	Oleaster
January	*Berberis japonica*	Japanese mahonia	Berberidaceae	Barberry
February	*Allium triquetrum*	Three-cornered leek	Amaryllidaceae	Amaryllis
February	*Stellaria media*	Chickweed	Caryophyllaceae	Pink
February	*Armoracia rusticana*	Horseradish	Brassicaceae	Cabbage
February	*Allium ursinum*	Wild garlic	Amaryllidaceae	Amaryllis
February	*Alliara petiolata*	Garlic mustard	Brassicaceae	Cabbage
March	*Glechoma hederacea*	Ground ivy	Lamiaceae	Mint
March	*Claytonia perfoliata*	Winter purslane	Montiaceae	Montiaceae
March	*Heracleum sphondylium*	Hogweed	Apiaceae	Carrot
March	*Arctium lappa*	Burdock	Asteraceae	Daisy
March	*Beta vulgaris* subsp. *maritima*	Sea beet	Amaranthaceae	Amaranth
April	*Magnolia* x *soulangeana*	Magnolia	Magnoliaceae	Magnolia

Month	Scientific name	Common name	Scientific name of family	Common name of family
April	*Urtica dioca*	Stinging nettle	Urticaceae	Nettle
April	*Fagus sylvatica*	Beech	Fagaceae	Beech
April	*Reynoutria japonica*	Japanese knotweed	Polygonaceae	Dock
April	*Prunus avium*	Cherry	Rosaceae	Rose
May	*Foeniculum vulgare*	Fennel	Apiaceae	Carrot
May	*Leucanthemum vulgare*	Ox-eye daisy	Asteraceae	Daisy
May	*Lamium album*	White dead nettle	Lamiaceae	Mint
May	*Mentha aquatica*	Water mint	Lamiaceae	Mint
May	*Nasturtium officinale*	Watercress	Brassicaceae	Cabbage
June	*Melissa officinalis*	Lemon balm	Lamiaceae	Mint
June	*Brassica nigra*	Black mustard	Brassicaceae	Cabbage
June	*Salicornia europaea*	Marsh samphire	Amaranthaceae	Amaranth
June	*Plantago maritima*	Sea plantain	Plantaginaceae	Plantain
June	*Atriplex portulacoides*	Sea purslane	Amaranthaceae	Amaranth
June	*Aster tripolium*	Sea aster	Asteraceae	Daisy
June	*Tropaeolum majus*	Nasturtium	Tropaeolaceae	Nasturtium
June	*Hemerocallis fulva*	Orange day lily	Xanthorrhoeaceae	Aloe
June	*Tilia cordata*	Common lime/linden	Malvaceae	Mallow
July	*Plantago lanceolata*	Ribwort plantain	Plantaginaceae	Plantain
July	*Diplotaxis tenuifolia*	Wild rocket, aka perennial wall rocket	Brassicaceae	Cabbage

Month	Scientific name	Common name	Scientific name of family	Common name of family
July	*Chenopodium album*	Fat hen	Amaranthaceae	Amaranth
July	*Blitum bonus-henricus*	Good King Henry	Amaranthaceae	Amaranth
July	*Atriplex prostrata*	Spear-leaved orache	Amaranthaceae	Amaranth
July	*Matricaria discoidea*	Pineapple weed	Asteraceae	Daisy
July	*Artemisia vulgaris*	Mugwort	Asteraceae	Daisy
August	*Filipendula ulmaria*	Meadowsweet	Rosaceae	Rose
August	*Rosa rugosa*	Japanese rose	Rosaceae	Rose
August	*Smyrnium olusatrum*	Alexanders	Apiaceae	Carrot
August	*Persicaria hydropiper*	Water pepper	Polygonaceae	Dock
August	*Origanum vulgare*	Wild marjoram	Lamiaceae	Mint
August	*Galium odoratum*	Sweet woodruff	Rubiaceae	Bedstraw
August	*Morus nigra*	Black mulberry	Moraceae	Mulberry/Fig
August	*Morus alba*	White mulberry	Moraceae	Mulberry/Fig
August	*Corylus avellana*	Hazel	Betulaceae	Birch
September	*Sambucus nigra*	Elder	Adoxaceae	Elder
September	*Boletus edulis*	Porcini	Boletaceae	Bolete
September	*Prunus cerasifera*	Cherry plum	Rosaceae	Rose
September	*Sorbus aucuparia*	Rowan	Rosaceae	Rose
September	*Malus* x *robusta*	Red sentinel crab apple	Rosaceae	Rose
September	*Rubus fruticosus*	Blackberry	Rosaceae	Rose
September	*Prunus domestica*	Wild plum	Rosaceae	Rose

Month	Scientific name	Common name	Scientific name of family	Common name of family
October	*Hydnum repandum*	Pied de mouton	Hydnaceae	Hydnaceae
October	*Geum urbanum*	Wood avens	Rosaceae	Rose
October	*Craterellus cornucopioides*	Horn of plenty	Cantharellaceae	Chanterelle
October	*Rosa canina*	Dog rose	Rosaceae	Rose
October	*Rumex acetosella*	Common sorrel	Polygonaceae	Dock
October	*Oxalis corniculata*	Procumbent yellow sorrel	Oxalidaceae	Wood sorrel
November	*Crataegus monogyna*	Hawthorn	Rosaceae	Rose
November	*Castanea sativa*	Sweet chestnut	Fagaceae	Beech
November	*Clitocybe nuda*	Wood blewit	Tricholomataceae	Funnel
November	*Lepista saeva*	Field blewit	Tricholomataceae	Blewit
November	*Pinus sylvestris*	Scots pine	Pinaceae	Pine
November	*Juniperus communis*	Juniper	Cupressaceae	Cypress
November	*Cydonia oblonga*	Quince	Rosaceae	Rose
December	*Craterellus tubaeformis*	Winter chanterelle	Cantharellaceae	Chanterelle
December	*Prunus spinosa*	Blackthorn	Rosaceae	Rose
December	*Achillea millefolium*	Yarrow	Asteraceae	Daisy
December	*Campanula portenschlagiana*	Wall bellflower	Campanulaceae	Bellflower
December	*Sanguisorba minor*	Salad burnet	Rosaceae	Rose
December	*Cardamine hirsuta*	Hairy bittercress	Brassicaceae	Cabbage
December	*Crataegus persimilis* 'Prunifolia'	Cockspur	Rosaceae	Rose

The basics of plant ID: learn fifty edible plants in ten minutes

Am I certain it's edible? Am I certain it won't harm me? Two basic questions the forager needs to answer when looking at any potentially edible plant. Once we decide to view the wild herbs, trees, mushrooms, seaweed and seafood of this country as a possible source of food, we enter a world not only brimming with exquisite and unusual flavours, textures and aromas, but also pitted with numerous hazards and even the vague possibility of death. Is it all worth it just for a plate of food? If approached sensibly then the answer is definitely yes. Approach this topic with too casual an attitude and the results may be very unpleasant.

So, that's the melodrama out of the way, now down to the simple bit – learning how to answer the two opening questions – and the easiest way to do this is to divide plants into their separate families, e.g. the Mint family, Cabbage family, Carrot family, allowing us to learn group characteristics (square or round stems, number and colour of petals, different leaf shapes, common smells, habitats). This in turn allows us to 'halfway' identify numerous plants very quickly – at least to be able to put them in the right family, which is a very good start on the road to correctly identifying them – and lets us know how we can proceed, depending on whether we have entered a family full of potential dangers or one with very few.

Imagine walking into your local pub: hopefully it contains your friends, some people who like you, and maybe a few who don't, but at least you know the protocol and can feel relatively at ease . . . this is the Mint family. Now let's go to that dodgy-looking bar on the other side of town. This is the Carrot family, full of dangers, full of delights and possible excitement, but whatever comes along it's the sort of place where we really need to tread carefully. In the same way, once we can positively identify the plant family we are looking at, we can adapt our behaviour accordingly. Here are a few of the most common plant families that our wild foods come from and a suggestion of how we should treat each one.

MINT FAMILY
Bar one, there are no poisonous members of this family in the UK although a few might taste horrid. A great place to start learning.

ROSE FAMILY
Almost all of our tree fruit and soft fruits come from this huge plant family with only a couple of toxic plants to avoid.

CABBAGE FAMILY
Numerous edible plants, none poisonous and a couple that taste pretty horrid. A safe place to learn.

CARROT FAMILY
Some deadly members like hemlock and some very tasty ones. Extreme caution is needed here. Not for beginners.

PEA FAMILY
Numerous edibles and a few poisonous members to be learnt and avoided.

DAISY FAMILY
Another huge group of plants, many edible, only a few toxic and some inedible, although a small minority of people are sensitive to plants in this family, which can cause allergic-type reactions on contact with the skin or when taken internally.

POTATO FAMILY
Dangerous members include deadly nightshade and various other extremely toxic plants.

BUTTERCUP FAMILY
A few edible and numerous poisonous plants.

LILY AND AMARYLLIS FAMILIES
Contains numerous tasty wild garlics and onions but also plenty of poisonous lilies. Careful study needed but great rewards on offer.

Some of the other plant families popular with foragers include the Poppy family, Mallow family, Dock family, Goosefoot family, Primrose family and Willow Herb family.

My first tip

I find the best way to learn is to concentrate on one family at a time; that's not to say it's not as rewarding and educational to just try to ID whatever you come across, I just find the repeat observation of similar characteristics is an excellent way to absorb information, and in addition it pays dividends to look at the same plant or plants at all times of their life cycle, throughout the year. Very often a small patch of land will contain various species from the same family and this is really useful for becoming familiar with their similarities as well as their differences.

My second tip

Bear in mind that often we want to collect a plant when some of its key ID features may not be on show, e.g. its flowers, or we may want to return to it to dig up its roots (but not in a London park) when there is very little of it left above ground, so being able to positively locate a plant by previously gathered information is very useful. I often refer to this as learning the plant backwards: making a 100 per cent positive ID when all the best information is on show, then revisiting it in all its stages in the safe knowledge that you know what it is.

My third tip

Mindfulness at all times. This book is not a comprehensive guide to the wild plants of the UK and for reliable identification it needs to be used with a volume that covers the specifics of plant ID in greater depth – a couple of suggestions are mentioned on pages 257–8 in point 5.

So, I promised fifty plants in less than ten minutes. Ready, steady . . . go! Welcome to the Mint family, also called the Dead Nettle family or, to give it its Latin name, Lamiaceae. This family not only contains numerous tasty wild herbs with great names like penny royal and bastard balm, but also many of our most common domestic ones: thyme, basil, sage, rosemary, lavender, marjoram and of course numerous types of mint. The only 'poisonous' plant here is called bugle (*Ajuga reptans*) and should be easy to spot/avoid with its dark green leaves and dark blue flowers.

The Mint family has plenty of easy features to help with identification but what do they all have in common? Well, a few things but maybe most obviously:

1. Smell

Does it smell like mint? Chances are that it is. Most, but not all, members of this group have quite strong, usually pleasant, occasionally unpleasant, smells. That's not to say that other plant families don't also have some strong smells but the Mint family has a few quite commonly reoccurring smells that will help you to narrow down your search. Smell is best used in tandem with some of the slightly more specific characteristics below but is often the only guide you need.

2. Stem shape

All members of this family have square stems. Get the stem between your thumb and forefinger and roll it. Each side has a flattish surface to it. This is an excellent ID feature but, as with smell, it doesn't mean you are definitely in the right family as there are other plant families with square stems. We will look at these in a minute and how to very easily, as the police say, 'eliminate them from our enquiries'.

3. Leaf arrangement

All members of this family have leaves in opposite and opposing pairs. In other words, there will be two leaves exactly opposite each other on either side of the stem, making a pair, further up the stem there will be another two leaves at right angles to the previous set, and so on all the way up the stem (this arrangement is called decussate). Get some mint from a garden or shop and have a look at this as well as the square stems. Numerous members of this family also have leaves with the similar pointed shape and serrated edges found on many nettles and mints. Not all do, but this is also a good indicator. Stinging nettles are not in this family and although they have decussate leaves and appear similar, the stems are rounded and ridged, not square.

4. Flowers

Using flowers for ID purposes is a bit of a luxury for the forager and means that some parts of the plant are well past their best (think how bitter many cabbage-like plants are when they have flowered or 'gone over'). The old name for the Mint family, Labiatae, comes from the Latin word *labium*, meaning lip, and refers to the two lobed/fused bottom petals of many of the flowers in this family. All flowers in this group have five petals that are fused together to create various united tube shapes, and although as foragers we want to avoid too much botany, it's worth mentioning that these flowers occur in various arrangements, many growing straight from the main stem (with no separate flower stems), like spearmint, and some growing in multiple layers above the rest of the plant, like lavender. Petal colour varies widely so this isn't helpful for general family ID but getting to recognize the sorts of flowers present in this family is easy and also useful.

5. Avoiding other similar families

I say similar but almost all of these bear little to no resemblance to members of the Mint family. Once we have an idea that we are in the right family, which, using just the first three of the methods above (to recap, that's 1. smell, 2. square stems, 3. decussate leaves) will take only a matter of seconds, it then requires a good ID book to help eliminate the other suspects. With a little practice this not only becomes very easy but also helps us to start learning new plant families. I use *The Wild Flower Key* by Francis Rose but there are many other good guides available and it's sensible practice to use more than one book and cross-reference. Please, do not trust the internet, especially when looking at photographs of plants, so many of which are incorrectly labelled. Thomas Elpel's book *Botany in a Day* is an excellent place to start and the information it includes is truly international, simply teaching how to recognize the group features or 'patterns' of all the common plant families.

Here are the possible lookalike families to avoid:

- Vervain family: With square stems and decussate leaves this is almost in the Mint family, but with only one wild UK species this is easy to ID with a good guide book.
- Purple Loosestrife family: Also just the one plant in this family in the UK (OK, two, but one grows in water). Stems and leaves similar to the mints but very different flowers.
- St John's Wort family: A couple with square stems and all with opposite/opposing leaves. Can look similar to young wild marjoram, but without the obvious smell these are easy to eliminate. Very different flowers, too.
- Figwort family: Half a dozen members with square stems and decussate leaf arrangement. Most with very different flowers or, if similar-looking to a mint flower, they will have three bottom lobes not two. A good ID book will help you pick these few up easily.
- Bedstraw family: Also have square stems, but their leaves occur in groups of four to eight in wheels (called whorls) around the stem. They also have flowers with four separate petals.

- Borage family: A few with square stems but the leaves are not opposite and opposing.
- Willow Herb family: Two or three with square stems but not opposite/opposing leaves.

As a footnote, the oil made from penny royal (*Mentha pulegium*) is extremely toxic but the plant in its unprocessed state is not, though still probably best avoided.

OK, STOP THE CLOCK. We can now reliably identify the fifty wild members of the Mint family we have in the UK. At this stage we're pretty much equipped with all the information we need to safely sample a tiny bit of the plant in question, happy in the knowledge that it belongs to a plant family with no potential dangers. Even so, it pays to only ever consume the smallest amount of any new food to be sure there is no adverse reaction, allergic or otherwise. Even the toxic bugle mentioned earlier has edible young leaves and young shoots (with reports of its narcotic effects, any more than a nibble is probably not a good idea, though). Although no other UK members of the Mint family are poisonous, some taste far too bitter to ever make it into a salad, and common sense and good practice require that rather than just having a nibble, it's very important to carry on to the final stages of ID below.

6. Habitat

It helps to become familiar with different habitats but this will come with time. Mints and their relatives grow in an enormously varied range of environments and, being perennial and often very hardy, can tolerate all sorts of conditions. Water mint is a great example of how habitat can help us specifically ID a plant. Does it look like mint? Does it smell like mint? Does it have the key ID features? Is it growing in or very close to water? It's water mint. Easy.

7. Fine-tuning your ID

Using a good guide, decent photos or illustrations and more specific details, we can put a plant into genus (a smaller group within the family) and then into species. This is the final stage of identification and would be written like this: *Mentha aquatica* (water mint) – *Mentha* describing the genus and *aquatica*, the species. Just for the record, these other plant families also have square stems but I really don't consider them lookalikes.

Safety, common sense and the law

First things first . . . NO NIBBLING!

Putting something in your mouth is not part of the identification process; it's what you do with food. Once you are 100 per cent certain of what you are dealing with, then trying a tiny amount may or may not be the appropriate next step, but tasting an unidentified plant is as dumb as putting a loaded gun in your mouth and pulling the trigger to find out if it contains bullets or not. In addition, it's dangerous to assume that just because one part of a plant is safe to eat, all other parts are, too. For example, numerous members of the Pea family (Leguminosae/Fabaceae), such as wisteria, have edible flowers but poisonous seeds, stems and leaves. Honeysuckle flowers, too, are edible while every other part of the plant is toxic, and plants you may be familiar with and assume are edible can turn out to be poisonous until cooked (elderberries in particular). Some plants, many of which are edible, contain sap that can irritate or damage the skin and eyes if picked carelessly. Some members of the Carrot family such as hogweed and wild parsnip contain biochemicals that become skin irritants (sometimes severely so) when the plant is damaged and it is exposed to strong sunlight.

All things in moderation

When trying something new for the first time, only eat a very small amount to make sure there are no adverse effects. We are all wired differently and can respond differently, too, so doing a simple tolerance test is a good habit to get into. By way of example, the root of common valerian is used to make a wonderful sedative tincture, rather like a natural valium. However, in about 10 per cent of people it has the polar opposite effect and acts as a stimulant. Although the Daisy family contains only a tiny number of toxic plants, some people have an intolerance to even small doses of thujone, an organic compound found in all members of this family. When trying a new species of mushroom for the first time, having obviously reached the point where I am utterly certain of my ID, I cook and eat a tiny section of one cap, the following day I eat a larger piece, and the day after is when I might consider consuming a whole portion.

Another reason for moderation is simply to not be too greedy. It's such a good feeling when you find and successfully identify something you know is going to taste great and it's sometimes really hard not to get carried away, but if foraging is to be accepted as a responsible urban activity it's vital that everyone involved doesn't overdo it. I'm not offering a lecture – I just wanted to mention it.

Pregnancy

As a general rule of thumb it's unwise to try anything new if you are pregnant, in case of any adverse effects on you or your baby. This applies even more so to wild food, some of which may contain chemical compounds that are fine when not pregnant but harmful if you are. For example, some pine needles can induce miscarriage in animals, some plants stimulate milk flow; numerous herbal remedies and pharmaceutical medicines are not recommended during pregnancy.

Dog poo and wee

The main danger to human health in dog faeces is the presence of the eggs of *Toxocara canis*. This is a parasitic worm that lives harmlessly in our furry friends but presents a danger to humans and can also spread by living in the soil long after the faeces have disappeared. Whether urban foraging or in the countryside, avoid dogs' muck and wash anything you find at ground level. Dog wee, due to clever canine leg cocking, may be on plants a good bit higher so I never eat anything as I go along unless I'm sure it's out of the dog-wee zone (how high can a wolf hound pee anyway?) or unless it's in an area I'm sure no dogs could access. Avoid plants that look scorched or blackening; this could be as a result of either animal urine or, far worse, the use of chemical pesticides. Just use your common sense and select plants, fruits, nuts and other foods in the same way you'd do in a shop, leaving behind anything that isn't in great condition. Lastly, and to overstate the obvious, don't pick anything from the base of city trees however healthy it looks (wee is a great source of nitrogen and plants thrive on it).

Always wash what you collect

Wash the plants and fruit you pick. I'm not suggesting you can't nibble the odd leaf or a few tasty edible berries as you go along, but as a general rule of thumb it makes good sense to wash the things you forage. Although washing cannot remove any toxins that have been absorbed into the plant's cells, it will remove any soil that might concentrate heavy metals, as well as any pesticide residue. Obviously, washing most flowers will damage them, which isn't a problem when making syrups or cordials, but might ruin the look of a lovely wild salad, so use your common sense. Because mushrooms are excellent at absorbing moisture, there are only a few species that I choose to give a quick rinse, instead preferring to brush them clean and cut off any dirty bits while I'm out and about.

Other animals and parasites

Birds, rats and foxes can't read those keep-out signs on the dog-free areas now available in most London parks, so use common sense to decide where you pick and what you eat.

Liver fluke is an unpleasant parasite found in livestock faeces. In its larval stage it attaches itself to plants in wet areas, predominantly riverbanks. Ingesting it can cause severe health problems, although reported cases of liver fluke in humans are extremely rare in the UK. Fortunately, it is killed and made totally harmless by cooking or briefly immersing in boiling water, so I always avoid eating raw any plants growing in rivers and ponds regardless of whether they can be traced back to land with livestock present or not.

Pollution and heavy metals

Many of the city's parks and commons have been green spaces for hundreds of years, often predating the industrial revolution and allowing us reliable documentary evidence of their history and usage. In my experience, the soil quality in many of these areas is very good, as indicated by the presence of various species of less-pollution-tolerant fungi, wild plant diversity and a lack of exposure to mass pesticides, more commonly used in rural agricultural areas. A recent study from Wellesley College in Boston totally defied the researchers' expectations, finding no difference in the levels of heavy metals on either peeled or unpeeled fruit from urban trees and rural orchards. More than that, they found the city fruit to contain 2.5 times the amount of calcium and higher levels of zinc, magnesium and potassium than the shop-bought equivalents.

Despite the information above, if foraging in built-up areas consider whether the plants may have absorbed pollution from close proximity to busy roads or heavy metals from poor, more industrialized areas of city soil. Mushrooms are excellent at absorbing pollutants so it is generally accepted that picking them close to busy roads is a bad idea (plus no one wants to get run over for a handful of fungi). I do not eat or recommend that anyone eats any city fungi; the underground organism that creates the mushrooms, mycelium, is excellent at absorbing any and all toxicity it encounters. I also recommend totally avoiding graveyards, where there are likely to be arsenic, lead and numerous other dangerous substances. As a rule of thumb, I don't eat any one city-foraged food from the same spot over a long period of time in case of any of these environment concerns. There is an ongoing debate about how safe it is to eat food grown or picked in urban areas, and obviously caution with all things wild or unknown is advisable, but there is so much rubbish in the foods we eat, harmful oestrogens in most packaging, pollution in the air, and a huge culture of drink, drugs and general stress in our cities that I see no harm in eating a few plants from one's local park. I suggest you do your own research and make up your own mind, but pay particular attention to the historic use of the land that you intend to forage on, which may, especially in an urban environment, not be as green as it first appears.

Poisonous plants and fungi

There are numerous toxic plants growing in this country. Once you decide to view the things growing around you as a potential source of food or medicine you are susceptible to various dangers and as such should only ever eat something you are 1,000 per cent sure of. Most of our common edibles have poisonous lookalikes, so I would advise at first only going foraging with someone knowledgeable or foraging with a good guidebook but not eating anything you find, to start with. With time and a little experience there is plenty you can pick and enjoy safely.

Common sense and the law

You are legally allowed to collect fruit, flowers, foliage and fungi for personal consumption, although obviously not from someone else's garden.

It is illegal to uproot any plant without permission of the landowner, and a civil offence to go onto land you don't own unless it's a public place, but don't get confused and imagine that a city park is common land, it's not . . . It's likely to be private property that you are granted access to and, as such, asked to behave by certain rules, some of which concern foraging, so it pays to be respectful of not only the environment but the people looking after it. Lastly, some plants are rare, protected and it is illegal to pick them, although this does not apply to any of the plants mentioned in this book.

Edible plants and their poisonous lookalikes

The process of becoming familiar with wild plants, whether edible or potentially harmful, is a long and careful one, and one that requires many encounters with the same species in all its different stages of development throughout the year (more about this in 'The basics of plant ID' section on page 251). Here we will look at ten of the edible plants featured in this book that that have equally common and often very similar lookalikes. These range from mildly toxic to deadly poisonous so, for obvious reasons, it is vital that you are able to tell the difference. Very often, one or two 'key features' will be enough to let you know whether you have made the correct identification, but novice foragers should never rely on single details and I strongly recommend that you cross reference your findings with two or three other books, or better still, show them to someone who is very experienced and whose opinion you totally trust. The illustrations below are simplistic and designed to make a few of the key features very obvious, or in the case of cow parsley versus hemlock, to show you just how similar they are. Although these drawings will help you spot some of the most obvious differences, do bear in mind that nature is full of variety and variation.

EDIBLE

Chickweed

POISONOUS

Scarlet Pimpernel

Although they appear to be very similar initially, these two plants are easy to tell apart by looking at the veins on the leaf. The chickweed leaf has numerous veins that branch off almost sideways to the side of the leaf, while the veins of the scarlet pimpernel are fewer and run very notably down the leaf towards the tip.

EDIBLE

Good King Henry

POISONOUS

Woody Nightshade

Note the almost triangular leaf shape of the Good King Henry versus the two separate and distinct lobes on the lower part of the woody nightshade leaf.

EDIBLE   POISONOUS

Cow Parsley   Hemlock

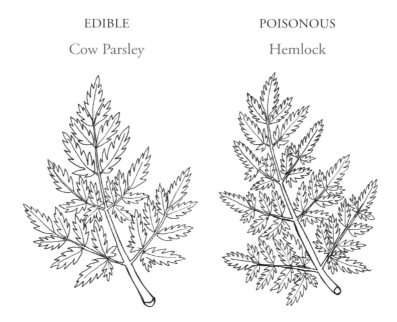

As you can see, the leaves of these two plants are almost identical.
It becomes much easier to tell them apart with experience, and as they
mature the differences in their botany becomes clearer, but initially
these are very tricky plants to ID, especially when they are young, as
are most members of the Carrot family. Can you spot the difference?
Look carefully at the shape of the leaf stem that is deeply grooved
in the cow parsley and almost totally round in the hemlock.
We will look at some other features below.

EDIBLE	POISONOUS
Cow Parsley	Hemlock

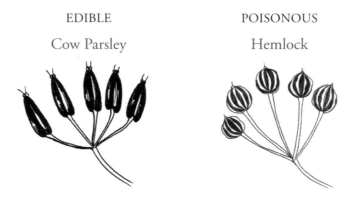

As you can see, the shape of the seeds are very different.

EDIBLE	POISONOUS
Cow Parsley	Hemlock

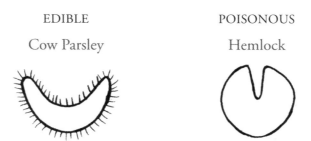

Here we are looking at the stems again, cut through in cross section. As you can see, the cow parsley is almost U-shaped, with a deep groove, similar to a stick of celery. It also has a covering of very tiny, fine hairs. The hemlock, on the other hand, has a totally round leaf stem, sometimes with, and often without, a very narrow groove. It has absolutely no hair on the leaf stem or any other part of the plant. There are various other ways to separate these plants, not least of all by their smell, which I discuss in more detail in January's 'cow parsley' entry (page 14). Lastly, the stems of the hemlock often have red/purple spotting on them and although a pinky-purple flush may be visible on the cow parsley, it will be a gentle tone and never appears like a spotty rash.

EDIBLE	POISONOUS
Common Sorrel	Lords and Ladies

Here the bottom of the sorrel leaf tips come to distinct points, as if they have been cut with scissors. The leaf tips of the lords and ladies, however, round off and never come to a sharp point. Although there are other differences to the leaf shape, and the lords and ladies is generally a darker, shinier green, this one specific point is sufficient to tell them apart.

EDIBLE

Fat Hen

POISONOUS

Black Nightshade

Black nightshade is considered by many to be an edible plant and is grown as a crop in some parts of the world. However, the levels of solanine (also present in green potatoes) that it contains appear to vary widely, so caution is advised. Fat hen, on the other hand, is a perfectly safe, extremely tasty variety of wild spinach, so it pays to be able to tell them apart, especially as they are often found growing together. The leaf of the fat hen is more upturned at the base than that of the black nightshade and has far more obvious and indented lobes. Additionally, it often appears to have a dull grey dusting to its surface, created by thousands of tiny vascular hairs.

EDIBLE   POISONOUS

Juniper   Yew

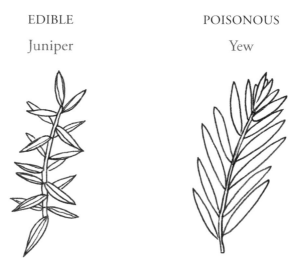

As you can see, the needles of the yew appear to be arranged in two rows, one either side of the leaf stem, in a fishbone pattern. They are also quite wide and rounded at the tip. The juniper has much sharper needles that come out of the stem at a variety of angles, creating the appearance of wheel spokes if viewed in cross section (as well as a much paler section running down each needle). Both can be found as trees or bushes but yew, which is extremely poisonous, is far more common and often used to make hedges, while the scarcer juniper has a distinct smell of gin to its crushed needles or berries.

EDIBLE

POISONOUS

Common Hogweed

Giant Hogweed

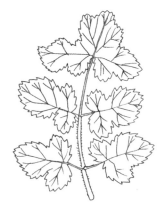

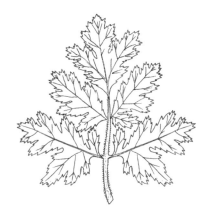

At first glance the leaves of both plants are quite similar but, as you can
see, the common hogweed has much rounder lobes to its leaves, while
the giant hogweed has much deeper, more indented lobes, the edges of
which are far more serrated than in its edible relative. Common hogweed
is a much gentler plant in general, with softer edges and texture, covered
in pale, soft to slightly bristly hairs. Giant hogweed, on the other hand,
is far more aggressive-looking, has a covering of dark, very stiff hairs and
dark red spotting all over the stem. When mature they are easy to tell
apart, the edible variety growing to about 1.5–2 metres, while the giant
hogweed can reach a mighty 5 metres high – a truly impressive wild
plant, but one that's sap can cause severe contact burns.

EDIBLE	POISONOUS
Common Hogweed	Giant Hogweed

Both plants produce disk-like seeds, flat ovals that are a few millimetres across but less than a millimetre thick. Although very similar, those of the common hogweed are noticeably more rounded than oval. These will appear only on mature plants at the latter stages of their life cycle, so the size of the plant will also be a good indication of the species.

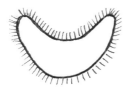

When cut into cross section, the leaf stem (not the main flowering stem) of the common hogweed has a wide groove (also found in cow parsley and celery) as well as a covering of soft, pale hairs. The giant hogweed has an almost round leaf stem with a deep channel-like groove and a covering of hard, dark hairs.

EDIBLE   POISONOUS

Alexanders   Hemlock Water Dropwort

The alexanders has a quite simple leaflet with one large top section
(called the terminal leaflet) and two smaller ones below. I think of it
as also having a slightly turquoise tinge to its shiny green foliage (not
everyone seems to see this, though). Hemlock water dropwort is not
only one of our most poisonous plants (if not the most), but it's also
extremely common and grows in damp places, wetlands, ditches and
river edges. Its leaves are more complex, more divided, and on closer
inspection are a different shape altogether, but caution is always needed
due to both plants growing in the same places, often intermingled.
Even touching this plant is not recommended. Alexanders is more of
a coastal plant but I see plenty of it thriving in the city these days.

EDIBLE

Alexanders

POISONOUS

Hemlock Water Dropwort

As you can see, these two plants have very different-shaped seeds.
The almost-black seeds of the alexanders occur in pairs, and together
they form the dark circles that are illustrated here, but come away from
the plant in two C-shaped halves. An excellent ID feature of these
hard little seeds is their strong, black pepper smell, easily
released by crushing one in the palm of your hand.

Acknowledgements

Enormous gratitude to Jason Irving for being my guide on all things botanical; it would have been a very different book without you. Needless to say any errors that remain are mine entirely.

I am grateful for the generosity, support and encouragement of the following people, without whom this book would probably not have happened: Ednyfed, Amanda, Beeka, Garry Eveleigh, Samar Hamman, Jamie Coleman, Lorna Driver-Davies, everyone at the Association of Foragers, the friends who have shared their knowledge and their recipes, and all the lovely people who have joined me on foraging walks over the years.

Grateful thanks also go to the following people for allowing me to reproduce their recipes:

Peter Studzinski, for allowing me to reproduce his cherry blossom syrup recipe. Rob McLeary, for finally giving up his pickled winter chanterelle recipe. Mark Williams at Galloway Wild Foods, for his inspirational wild sushi ideas. Garry Eveleigh, for allowing me to reproduce the wild mushroom risotto cakes recipe from his book *The Wild Cook*. Adele Nozedar, for allowing me to reproduce the water mint ice cream from her book *The Hedgerow Handbook*. Katherine Taylor, for allowing me to reproduce her candied ginger recipe. Robin Harford at www.eatweeds.co.uk, for allowing me to adapt his elder and clove cordial. Lorna Driver-Davies at Feel Better Nutrition, for the super-immune-boosting soup recipe.

And lastly, thanks to the lovely staff and wonderful coffee at Cinnamon Village cafe, where a large amount of this book was written.

Index

Note: page numbers in **bold** refer to illustrations.